GOD
Gave
WINE

OTHER BOOKS BY KENNETH L. GENTRY, JR.

The Christian Case Against Abortion
The Christian and Alcoholic Beverages
The Charismatic Gift of Prophecy: A Reformed Response to
    Wayne Grudem
The Beast of Revelation
Before Jerusalem Fell: Dating the Book of Revelation
House Divided: The Break-up of Dispensational Theology (with
    Greg Bahnsen)
The Greatness of the Great Commission: The Christian Enterprise
    in a Fallen World
He Shall Have Dominion: A Postmillennial Eschatology
Lord of the Saved: Getting to the Heart of the Lordship Debate
God's Law in the Modern World: The Continuing Relevance
    of Old Testament Law
The Great Tribulation: Past or Future? (with Thomas D. Ice)
Revelation: A Tale of Two Cities

CHAPTERS FOUND IN COLLECTED WORKS

"Charities Should Care for the Poor" in David L. Bender, ed.
    The Welfare State: Opposing Viewpoints
Three chapters in Gary North, ed. *Theonomy: An Informed*
    Response
"The Preterist View" in Marvin Pate, ed. *Four Views on the*
    Book of Revelation
"The Postmillennial View" in Darrell Bock, ed. *Three Views on*
    the Millennium and Beyond
"The Case for the Preterist Approach to Revelation" in David
    A. Hagopian, ed. *Always Reforming: A Dialogue of Differences*
    within the Reformed Tradition
"A Revelation of the Revelation," and "Theonomy and
    Confession" in Robert R. Booth, ed. *Greg L. Bahnsen*
    Festschrift

GOD
Gave
WINE

*What the Bible
says about Alcohol*

KENNETH L. GENTRY, JR.

Oakdown™
Lincoln, California

For a catalog of education materials produced by Dr. Kenneth L. Gentry, Jr., contact him at: kennethgentry@cs.com.

Publisher's Cataloging-in-Publication

Gentry, Kenneth L.
    God gave wine : what the Bible says about alcohol /
Kenneth L. Gentry, Jr. -- 1st ed.
    p. cm.
    Includes bibliographical references.
    LCCN: 00133628
    ISBN: 0-9700326-6-8
    "A smaller version of this book was originally
published under the title: The Christian and alcoholic
beverages : a Biblical perspective (Grand Rapids :
Baker, 1986)"--T.p. verso.

    1. Temperance--Biblical teaching. 2. Alcoholic
beverages--Biblical teaching. I. Title.

HV5183.G46 2000   241'.681
                    QBI00-825

Published by Oakdown™ (www.oakdown.com),
of MenschWerks™ (www.menschwerks.com)
P.O. Box 910 • Lincoln, CA 95648

To my wife,
Melissa,

for your love is better than wine.
Song of Songs 1:2

TABLE OF CONTENTS

Preface

1. Introductory Matters   1

2. The Bible and Alcohol Abuse   17

3. The Old Testament and Alcohol Use   33

4. The New Testament and Alcohol Use   67

5. Alleged Negative Passages   83

6. Bible Teaching on Christian Liberty   105

7. Common Objections Considered   131

8. Conclusion   147

    Chapter Citations   151

    References Used   157

PREFACE

The volume you have before you is an updated, greatly expanded edition of my earlier book entitled *The Christian and Alcoholic Beverages: A Biblical Perspective*. The original was published by Baker in 1986 and went through two printings. Since it has been out of print for almost a decade, I have received numerous requests for it. I am thankful to Dennis Miller and Joel Miller at Oakdown™ Books for republishing it in this new, enlarged format. I trust that the expansion of the material will enhance the usefulness of the book in the continuing debate.

The first edition of the work was well received by many, enjoying several encouraging reviews. Reviews appeared in *The Journal of the Evangelical Theological Society, Pro Rege, Librarian's World, Bookstore Journal, The PCA Messenger, The Counsel of Chalcedon, The Moderationist Reader, The Bookshelf,* and other publications. In addition, I was interviewed on several regional Christian radio programs about my position. Needless to say, some of the call-ins after the interview were quite lively!

Of course, as you might expect, *The Christian and Alcoholic Beverages* was also vigorously opposed by many. Some of the callers to the talk shows became downright irate, despite my attempt reasonably, biblically, and gently to present the moderationist viewpoint. One of the most unusual reviews appeared in *The Christian Statesman*. In fact, it was *not* a review of my book, but a review of a *review* of it!

That "review" opened with these words: "I haven't seen this book, nor have I been persuaded to buy it." The remainder of his review amply proved he had not read the book. This sort of response — dismissal without consideration — is a patent illustration of how emotionally charged the debate over wine drinking can be. It also demonstrates how disinterested some are to examine the biblical evidence.

The purpose of this study is *not* to encourage anyone to drink. Why would I care whether or not someone drinks wine? In fact, *I* do not even drink it! Rather, its purpose is three-fold: (1) Methodological: to illustrate the proper biblical method in biblical research. (2) Ethical: to demonstrate the biblical position on this volatile moral issue. (3) Apologetical: to defend the coherence of the biblical revelation, which some believe is disjointed on this question.

Since the question of drinking is so hotly debated, I wanted (hopefully) to impart a dose of calm biblical reflection into the discussion. Hopefully, you the reader will see that — whether you agree or not with my *conclusions* — at least my presentation tries carefully to analyze the Bible in resolving the issue. Whether I am successful or not, of course, depends on the cogency of my scriptural arguments. I certainly have attempted to deal with the leading biblical passages touching on the question, as well as to respond to the leading advocates opposing my viewpoint.

I must thank my good friend Michael Jacques for his help in this project. He carefully double-checked all the Scripture references for me. With so many references, typos can become a real nuisance. Michael is a constant source of encouragement to me through his consistent attendance at, and service in, the church of which I am pastor, Grace Orthodox Presbyterian Church, Costa Mesa, California (www.grace-opc.org).

May the Lord be pleased to bless the publication of this study for the strengthening of his people's worldview.

Kenneth L. Gentry, Jr., Th.D.
Bahnsen Theological Seminary
Placentia, California
January 2001

CHAPTER 1
INTRODUCTORY MATTERS

He causes the grass to grow for the cattle,
And vegetation for the labor of man,
That he may bring forth food from the earth,
And wine which makes man's heart glad.

Psalm 104:14-15

Few issues relating to the Christian walk tend to stir more deep-seated feelings and generate more heated debate than the Christian approach to alcoholic beverages. Expectations regarding this issue have divided Christians "in sundry times and divers manners." Surely, "the wine and the many" is a continuing ethical problem in the church and society.

In the last two hundred years in America virtually every branch of the Church has been drawn into the debate over alcohol. Two of the early leaders sparking the modern temperance movement in the late eighteenth and early nineteenth centuries were Dr. Benjamin Rush and Rev. John Marsh. Rush, a signer of the Declaration of Independence and a renowned physician, laid the foundation for what would later become a full-fledged temperance movement, when in 1784 he published his booklet, *An Inquiry Into the Effects of Ardent Spirits on the Mind and Body.* Later Rev. Marsh became the catalyst for a self-sustaining movement when he published his anti-alcohol lecture, "Putnam and the Wolf," in 1829. By 1833 Marsh had established the first National Temperance Convention in Philadelphia.

This impassioned debate over "ardent spirits" not only resulted in educational temperance movements from within Christian circles, but eventually led to constitutional prohibition in the nation at large.[1] On January 16, 1919, the 18th Amendment to the U. S. Constitution was officially adopted, and on January 17, 1920, the Volstead Act implemented it. After much social and legal chaos this amendment was repealed on December 5, 1933, by the 21st Amendment.

Despite the failure of Prohibition the battle still rages within Christian circles. In fact, as Mark A. Noll observes, "some evangelicals have made opinion on liquor more important for fellowship and cooperation ... than attitudes toward the person of Christ or the nature of salvation."[2]

The issue of wine drinking so inflames some Christians that emotional reaction threatens to silence both the Word of God and to diminish the evidence of medical science: "There is something deep within me that cries out against even the thought that Christ Jesus ever drank or produced alcoholic beverages. If I had no Scripture or scientific evidence to support me, what I have seen with my own eyes — and what I feel in my heart — would be enough."[3] This writer's alarm is so profound that he "seriously doubt[s] Christians who drink can be called saints. I call them 'sipping saints,' only because they are self-confessed Christians who drink."[4] Another popular evangelist flatly declares, "Everyone who drinks has an alcohol problem."[5]

This emotional reaction against alcohol so possesses the minds of some that for Christian ministers to tolerate it provides evidence of an approaching Antichrist and one world church. Reflecting upon a Navy chaplain's suggestion that wine be employed in communion due to the difficulty of preserving grape juice on long ocean voyages, one writer laments, "I now believe it to have been the result of false ecumenism, designed to lead all who profess Christianity to the same ill advised practices. This, I believe, was a step toward the great ecumenical unorthodox church which some see predicted in Matthew 24:24 [Jesus' famous last-days passage]."[6] The author goes on to argue "the inference is inescapable that God holds in contempt preachers who preach in favor of alcoholic beverages even in normal times."[7]

I well know the heat of passion radiating from the debate. As a Bible major at the fundamentalist Tennessee Temple College in the early 1970s, I accepted my teachers' anti-wine interpretation of the biblical record. Later, after "I saw the lite" of the biblical evidence allowing alcoholic beverages, I released the first edition of this book (1986). Immediately, Christian friends began to confront me with "shock and dismay" about my "dangerous" views. Yet, here I stand. And once again, I present the biblical argument with the call: "Come, let us reason together."

THREE VIEWS IN THE DEBATE

Basically three classic positions prevail on the question of drink. In the study following I will label these the *prohibitionist*, the *abstentionist*, and the *moderationist* views.

The *prohibitionist* position maintains that Christians should universally avoid alcoholic beverages as unfit for human consumption, being specifically forbidden by Scripture. Some prohibitionists regard alcoholic beverages themselves to be "innately sinful."[8] Since "this substance ... at the last 'bites like a serpent and stings like an adder' [is it] not inherently evil.'"[9] Others deem the act of partaking them to be immoral.

Presenting the prohibitionist position are the following works: Stephen M. Reynolds, *Alcohol and the Bible* and *The*

Biblical Approach to Alcohol; Jack Van Impe, *Alcohol: The Beloved Enemy*; David Wilkerson, *Sipping Saints*; and Robert P. Teachout's doctoral dissertation, "The Use of 'Wine' in the Old Testament."

In the foreword to Van Impe's *Alcohol: the Beloved Enemy*, Teachout — with italicized emphasis — forthrightly declares, *"Alcohol is never approved of by God in any amount for the obedient Christian."*[10] Stephen Reynolds agrees: "It is the intent of this book to prove that Proverbs teaches an absolute prohibition against the beverage use of alcohol."[11] Wilkerson warns, "Christians who drink alcoholic beverages of any kind are deceiving themselves."[12] In this view the question of alcohol is a "legal" matter; it is absolutely forbidden by the Law of God.

Dr. Reynolds is undoubtedly the most learned (he holds a Ph.D. in Semitic Languages from Princeton University) and the most vigorous proponent of prohibition (he has published two books on the subject vehemently criticizing the use of alcohol). Consequently, I will give his work special attention.

In fact, Reynolds so vigorously opposes any alcohol consumption that he points to Micah 2:11 as a warning. This passage reads, "If a man walking after wind and falsehood had told lies and said, 'I will speak out to you concerning wine and liquor,' he would be spokesman to this people." Reynolds argues that this passage speaks of "the proper degree of contempt God has for the opinion of people, specifically in the circumstances in which the prophet spoke, who would be eager to accept the preaching of a man approving the consumption of alcoholic wine."[13] Indeed, "the inference is inescapable that God holds in contempt preachers who preach in favor of alcoholic beverages even in normal times."[14]

The *abstentionist* view maintains that although Scripture does not expressly forbid alcoholic beverages in toto, alcohol consumption *in our society today* is nevertheless imprudent and should not be condoned. This is due to both the loose moral standards of today and the easy availability of highly alcoholic beverages (technology has increased alcoholic potency). In this view, abstinence is not a matter of "law" but of love. Thus, the Christian should *voluntarily* forgo alcohol consumption as a matter of prudence and concern.

Gleason Archer draws a clear distinction between this view and the prohibitionist one: "If we really care about the souls of men, and if we are really in business for Christ rather than for ourselves, then there seems (to this writer, at least) to be no alternative to total abstinence — not as a matter of legalism, but rather as a matter of love."[15]

Representing the abstentionist position is the report published by the Reformed Presbyterian Church, Evangelical Synod's "Study Committee on the Beverage Use of Alcohol Report."[16] In a news release summarizing this report, we read, "In light of the increasing serious abuse of alcohol in contemporary American culture, the Synod reaffirms its advocacy of total abstinence from the beverage use of alcohol.... This is a matter of prudence based on the exercise of Christian love, in our contemporary American culture.... It should be acknowledged that Scripture neither makes total abstinence a mark of holiness nor a universal requirement."[17]

Other published defenses of abstentionism include: Harold Lindsell, *The World, the Flesh and the Devil*; Gleason L. Archer, *Encyclopedia of Bible Difficulties*; Jerry G. Dunn, *The Christian in a Drinking Society*; and R. Laird Harris, *The Bible and Wine*.

After surveying various statistics, Lindsell forcefully presses this viewpoint:

> When one considers these statistics and ponders the
> numerous drawbacks to the use of alcohol, it remains for
> those who advocate its use to demonstrate its value and
> benefits. There is no argument in its favor that is not out-
> weighed by the drawbacks.... In view of the facts, the case
> for abstinence now seems to go beyond the simple question
> of expediency to the direct issue of principle.... It is not
> difficult to conclude that abstinence is to be preferred even
> though there is no express prohibition in Scripture against
> the use of alcohol in moderation.[18]

Dunn more insistently presses the biblical necessity:
"There is a strong scriptural basis for total abstinence for
the Christian."[19]

The *moderationist* view maintains that alcoholic beverages
are permitted to Christians if moderately consumed and in a
circumspect manner. This is the view I endorse and will
defend in the following pages.

Representative defenses of this view include: G. I.
Williamson, *Wine in the Bible and the Church*; Andre Bustanoby,
The Wrath of Grapes; J. G. Vos, *The Separated Life*; and my own
previously published work, *The Christian and Alcoholic Beverages*
— the first edition of the present re-titled and expanded
work. For an insightful published debate see: Kenneth L.
Gentry, Jr. and Stephen M. Reynolds, "Does Scripture Permit
Us to Drink Alcoholic Beverages?"[20]

SIGNIFICANCE OF THE DEBATE

The issue before us is an important one that merits
serious consideration by concerned Christians. The
implications of the question are many and varied. I will briefly
allude to three in introducing the study.

First, the issue has important ramifications for both the
individual's *personal witness* and his *Christian counsel.* As
redeemed vessels of mercy (1 Cor. 6:19-20; Titus 2:11-14),

God obligates Christians to self-consciously live out every aspect of their lives to the glory of God: "Whether, then, you eat or drink or whatever you do, do all to the glory of God" (1 Cor. 10:31). "Whatever you do in word or deed, do all in the name of the Lord Jesus, giving thanks through Him to God the Father" (Col. 3:17).

Since the alcohol question will not simply go away — it has been a raging debate for 200 years — the Christian should be ready to give a biblical answer to any who may inquire into his position and practice regarding drinking. We should do so both to defend and to enhance our Christian witness. Furthermore, circumstances may call upon us to provide biblically based counsel to those troubled over the matter, for whatever reasons.

Second, the issue has serious implications regarding both the church's *ecclesiastical integrity* and her *spiritual unity.* The troublesome issue of wine drinking continues to generate vigorous disagreement within Christian churches, often leading to strife and contention. Rather than tolerating divisions of this sort (1 Cor. 1:11; 3:1-3), Scripture calls Christians to unity in the Spirit:

> For even as the body is one and yet has many members, and all the members of the body, though they are many, are one body, so also is Christ. For by one Spirit we were all baptized into one body, whether Jews or Greeks, whether slaves or free, and we were all made to drink of one Spirit. For the body is not one member, but many. (1 Cor. 12:12-14)

> I, therefore, the prisoner of the Lord, entreat you to walk in a manner worthy of the calling with which you have been called, with all humility and gentleness, with patience, showing forbearance to one another in love, being diligent to preserve the unity of the Spirit in the bond of peace. (Eph. 4:1-3)

But we must base this unity of faith and practice upon a sure foundation of truth. Christ our Lord prays for us: "Sanctify them in the truth; Your word is truth" (John 17:17). Paul encourages us: "We are no longer to be children, tossed here and there by waves, and carried about by every wind of doctrine, by the trickery of men, by craftiness in deceitful scheming; but speaking the truth in love, we are to grow up in all aspects into Him, who is the head, even Christ" (Eph. 4:14-15). Consequently, members and leaders of a church must promote a truth-based unity on this and all other issues.

Third, the issue has implications regarding both the church's *social outreach* and her *cultural influence*.[†] The Bible calls Christians to be "the light of the world" (Matt. 5:14-16) in order to expose the "deeds of darkness" (Eph. 5: 11). To give proper and consistent guidance to the world regarding alcohol use requires that we have our biblical facts straight. Otherwise, we are providing little more than common-sense notions of righteousness. We can demand neither more nor less than God's Word allows. After all, Scripture commands us to "take every thought captive to the obedience of Christ" (2 Cor. 10:5) — and Christ speaks to us in the objective, propositional revelation of Scripture.

† For a helpful summary of the question of drink in Scripture and in historical church practice, see: "Alcoholism" in Harrison, *Encyclopedia of Biblical and Christian Ethics*. For a concise presentation of the issue of social drinking, see the same work under the entry, "Drinking, Social."

STRUCTURE OF THE PRESENTATION

I designed the present study for exploring the two fundamental questions involved in the whole debate: First, what is the express teaching of Scripture on the *morality* of alcohol consumption? Second, what is the express teaching of Scripture on the *practicality* of alcohol consumption?

After a brief chapter noting the reprehensible nature of alcohol *abuse* (Chapter 2), Chapters 3 through 5 will especially expose the error of the prohibitionist position, while Chapter 6 will demonstrate the practical shortcomings of the abstentionist view. In all of this, I will be providing evidence supporting the moderationist practice.

Of course, these two primary questions do not exhaust the material of Christian ethical concern regarding the alcohol question. Among other important matters worthy of consideration are the following:

1. *The theological implications of each of the three positions.* The theology of Scripture is a "seamless garment,"† providing a coherent, unified message. Consequently, biblical teachings regarding creation, revelation, Christ, salvation, ecclesiology, and other doctrines are necessarily impacted in the debate. For instance, according to some, alcoholic beverages are inherently evil, a belief which affects our understanding of the doctrine of creation. Other opponents of fermented drink suggest that the Bible is intentionally unclear on its prohibition, thereby serving as a "test" of one's perception, a notion which impacts the perspicuity of Scripture, as well as the nature of sanctification. Still others hold that consuming alcohol is itself sinful, which should cause us to wonder about the nature of Christ's miracle of turning water into wine — wine which was clearly meant to be consumed.

† See the writings of Cornelius Van Til for an in-depth exposition of this important truth. For an introduction to the "interdependence of biblical doctrines" from a Van Til perspective, see: Frame, 295-332. For the clearest summary and presentation of Van Til's system, see: Bahnsen, *Van Til's Apologetic.*

2. *The internal logical consistency of each of the three positions.* In that God is the God of order (1 Cor. 14:33) and of reason (Is. 1:18), we must be careful to avoid potential logical fallacies resulting from the manner in which we argue our positions.

Later I will provide a few logical syllogisms illustrating some pitfalls we must avoid in the ethical debate. I will not, however, engage in a full-scale internal critique of the logical coherence of the various positions.

3. *The health impact of each of the three positions.* Important practical questions arise in our debate: Is alcohol consumption necessarily debilitating? May we prescribe alcohol for some people with certain physiological conditions (1 Tim. 5:23; Prov. 31:6), while forbidding it to others with contrary health concerns? For instance, I have a liver condition called non-alcoholic steatohepititis which prevents my partaking of alcoholic drinks.† Though I will not focus on such issues, I will touch briefly upon them in Chapter 7, because medical considerations are often of major concern for the prohibitionist position.

† I should note, however, as I did in a 1994 radio debate with George Ormsby, that I personally do not care much for alcoholic beverages. At the time, I seldom consumed more than four or five glasses of wine in an entire year.

4. *The socio-cultural impact of each of the three positions.* I should note as well that demographic studies and sociological statistics are often helpful for putting the matter in contemporary perspective. My omitting such statistical studies is due partly to their ready availability elsewhere‡ and partly to the generally well-known impact of alcohol abuse. Certainly, *all* Christian positions on the question of drink deplore the *abuse* of alcohol and find sociological analyses helpful for portraying the problem. Yet, they too are of secondary importance to the heart of the issue: What saith the Scripture?

‡ See, for instance: *Seventh Special Report to the U. S. Congress on Alcohol and Health*, published by the National Institute on Alcohol Abuse and Alcoholism; Siegel, et al. eds., *Illegal Drugs and Alcohol; Prevention Plus II*, from the Office for Substance Abuse Prevention; Scott Barbour, ed., *Alcohol: Opposing Viewpoints*.

THE BIBLE AND CHRISTIAN ETHICS

Let us now turn to a *scriptural* analysis of the question of alcoholic beverages. The starting point for developing a truly Christian ethical system must be the study of Scripture itself. The evangelical, born-again Christian confidently holds that God's holy will is the perfect standard of righteousness. And he further trusts that God's will is authoritatively, unchangeably, and infallibly revealed in the Scriptures of the Old and New Testaments. Consequently, the Bible — and the Bible alone — must be the starting point and supreme standard for defining truly Christian ethical behavior.

In the venerable Westminster Confession of Faith (hereinafter WCF) we find a beautiful declaration of the pre-eminency of Scripture as the standard for faith and life:

> Therefore it pleased the Lord, at sundry times and in divers manners, to reveal Himself, and to declare that his will unto his Church; and afterwards, for the better preserving and propagating of the truth, and for the more sure establishment and comfort of the Church against the corruption of the flesh, and the malice of Satan and of the world, to commit the same wholly unto writing: which maketh the holy Scripture to be most necessary; those former ways of God's revealing his will unto his people being now ceased. (WCF 1:1)

The Scripture is God's revealed and permanent will for man (Deut. 12:32; Is. 8:20; Rom. 3:1-4). Because of this, evangelical Christian thought insists upon two important ethical principles:

1. *The ubiquity of ethics.* That is, because man is a moral creature created in the image of God (Gen. 1:26-27; 9:6), *everything* a man does has moral implications (Ps. 139:1-12; Prov. 15:3; 1 Cor. 10:31; 2 Cor. 5:10).

2. *The sufficiency of Scripture.* That is, although God did

not reveal detailed responses to each and every possible act of man, nevertheless, Scripture provides express precepts and general principles that adequately govern every contingency (Deut. 8:3b; Ps. 119:105; 2 Tim. 3:16-17).

Again we would do well to note the emphatic and pointed declaration of the Westminster Confession of Faith in this regard: "The whole counsel of God concerning all things necessary for his own glory, man's salvation, faith, and life, is either expressly set down in Scripture, or by good and necessary consequence may be deduced from Scripture: unto which nothing at any time is to be added, whether by new revelations of the Spirit, or traditions of men" (WCF 1:6). Thus, we may confidently and boldly assert that "the supreme judge by which all controversies of religion are to be determined, and all decrees of councils, opinions of ancient writers, doctrines of men, and private spirits, are to be determined, and in whose sentence we are to rest, can be no other but the Holy Spirit speaking in the Scripture" (WCF 1:10).

These doctrinal affirmations themselves flow from the express teaching of Scripture itself: "All Scripture is inspired by God and profitable for teaching, for reproof, for correction, for training in righteousness, that the man of God may be adequate, equipped for every good work" (2 Tim. 3:16-17). To the apostles — who were divinely commissioned and supernaturally gifted bearers of the revelation of God — the Lord Jesus Christ promised: "But when He, the Spirit of truth, comes, He will guide you into all the truth" (John 16:13). God's Word is unequivocal truth (Ps. 119:160; John 17:17; Rom. 3:4), just as Jesus Christ is the personification of God's Word (John 1:1; 1 John 1:1; Rev. 19:13) and truth (John 1:17; 14:6). Therefore, God requires us to bring "every thought captive to the obedience of Christ" (2 Cor. 10:5).

That is, we must submit every area of life to Christ and his will as revealed in Scripture (Rom. 12:2).

In the intellectual and spiritual climate of our times, numerous examples of deviating from the norm of Scripture exist. For example, perhaps the foundational heresy of Mormonism is its belief in an open canon which allows for continued "revelation" from God (*The Book of Mormon*, *The Doctrine and Covenants*, *The Pearl of Great Price*, and so on). For example, 2 Nephi 29:3-10 in *The Book of Mormon* reads:

> Many of the Gentiles shall say: A Bible! A Bible! We have got a Bible, and there cannot be any more Bible. But thus saith the Lord God: ... Thou fool, that shall say: A Bible, we have got a Bible, and we need no more Bible.... Wherefore murmur ye, because that ye shall receive more of my word? ... Because that ye have a Bible ye need not suppose that it contains all my words; neither need ye suppose that I have not caused more to be written.

Similarly, the ever-present danger in Pentecostalism and the charismatic movement lies in their frequent claims to continuing direct access to the mind of God. This allegedly comes through supernatural and miraculous revelatory gifts of the Holy Spirit, such as prophetic utterances, divine visions, and heavenly tongues. For instance, J. Rodman Williams writes:

> In prophecy God speaks. It is as simple, and profound, and startling as that! What happens in the fellowship is that the word may suddenly be spoken by anyone present, and so variously, a "Thus says the Lord" breaks forth in the fellowship.... Many of us also had convinced ourselves that prophecy ended with the New Testament (despite all the New Testament evidence to the contrary), until suddenly through the dynamic thrust of the Holy Spirit prophecy comes alive again. Now we wonder how we could have misread the New Testament for so long![21]

Finally, the clear error of neo-orthodoxy is its denial of propositional truth. This particular theological view prefers subjectivism to objective revelation. That is, dynamic revelation, confrontational crises, and so forth prevail over propositional truth. By way of example, Karl Barth holds that "the Bible is God's Word so far as God lets it be his Word."[22]

These widely divergent camps suffer from a common malady: subjectivism in determining the will of God. Unfortunately, even conservative fundamentalism often borders on this error in its ethical reliance upon "the leading of the Holy Spirit" divorced from the Word of God — sign-seeking, special guidance by direct feelings and impressions of the Holy Spirit, and the like.[†] And this error is particularly relevant to the issue at hand because resistance to alcohol often appears devout and "biblical."

† For a helpful corrective, see: Freisen and Maxson, *Decision Making and the Will of God: A Biblical Alternative to the Traditional View.*

We are greatly tempted to resort to "sanctified feelings" or "holy common sense" for resolving complex ethical issues, instead of turning to the Word of God itself — especially in our day of instant-this and freeze-dried-that.

What the world so needs today — second only to regeneration itself — is a coherent, biblically derived ethical system by which to judge all thought and behavior — one that rests on Scripture alone. Autonomous ethics are internally contradictory (because they are not true) and inherently evil (because they deny God). A truly Christian ethic arises from the Word of the Living God (John 17:17) — not the traditions of men, whether "secular" or "religious" (Matt. 15:3, 6; Mark 7:13). The abiding strength of a truly vital Christianity derives from its sole reliance upon the sufficiency of Scripture for all matters concerning faith and practice. The inspired, infallible, inerrant Word of God is and must always be the regulating principle of Christian thought and conduct. Theologian R. B. Kuiper well states this precept: "All Christian teachings, whether doctrinal or ethical, are drawn from the Bible. According to Christianity the acid test of truth and goodness is Scripturalness."[23]

With these things in mind, we may now approach the particular problem of "grape expectations," as my friend Jeff Ventrella puts it. Because millions of people drink alcoholic beverages, how are we to resolve the question of the "wine and the many"? Since the material of the Christian ethical position must be that of Scripture, the question then is, as stated previously: What does the Scripture teach about the consumption of alcoholic beverages? May Christians be, in fact, promise drinkers?

CHAPTER 2

THE BIBLE AND ALCOHOL ABUSE

Having laid down the foundational principle of ethical inquiry, we may now consider the question at hand. Let us begin our formal inquiry by noting first that Scripture clearly deems drunkenness a sinful state meriting God's disapproval and anger. Each of the three Christian positions on the use of wine condemns alcohol abuse and dependence. In fact, the Scripture unsparingly condemns drunkenness, frequently and from a variety of angles. I will cover eight classes of scriptural condemnation of alcohol *abuse*. This should allay any fears that the moderationist position is unconcerned with drunkenness and alcohol dependency.

1. EXPRESSLY CONDEMNED

Scattered throughout the Bible are the following objective, non-debatable condemnations of alcohol abuse. These prohibitions are quite clear, and several involve most severe denunciations ranging from the outpouring of divine woes to disbarring one from the kingdom of God:

> Woe to the proud crown of the drunkards of Ephraim,
> And to the fading flower of its glorious beauty,
> Which is at the head of the fertile valley
> Of those who are overcome with wine! (Is. 28:1)

Do not get drunk with wine. (Eph. 5:18)

Let us behave properly as in the day, not in carousing and drunkenness. (Rom. 13:13)

Now the deeds of the flesh are evident, which are: immorality, impurity, sensuality ... envyings, drunkenness, carousings, and things like these, of which I forewarn you just as I have forewarned you that those who practice such things shall not inherit the kingdom of God. (Gal. 5:19, 21)

[Neither] thieves, nor the covetous, nor drunkards ... shall inherit the kingdom of God. (1 Cor. 6:10)

Due to the severe nature of such strong condemnations, the Christian must even avoid fellowshipping with the drunkard. Proverbs exhorts, "Do not be with heavy drinkers of wine, or with gluttonous eaters of meat" (Prov. 23:20). Ezekiel poetically portrays the evil comradeship associated with drunkards: "And the sound of a carefree multitude was with her; and drunkards were brought from the wilderness with men of the common sort. And they put bracelets on the hands of the women and beautiful crowns on their heads" (Ezek. 23:42).

Speaking in a parable, Christ illustrates evil as involving fellowship with drunkards: "And he shall begin to beat his fellow slaves and eat and drink with drunkards" (Matt. 24:49). Paul legislates the new covenant response: "I wrote to you not to associate with any so-called brother if he should be an immoral person, or covetous, or an idolater, or a reviler, or a drunkard, or a swindler — not even to eat with such a one" (1 Cor. 5:11).

Clearly, Scripture resolutely condemns the abuse of alcoholic beverages.

2. IS A CURSE ON MAN

Not only does Scripture forbid drunkenness by direct pronouncement, but the presence of drunkenness in a society manifests the very wrath and curse of God. Indeed, drunkenness can serve as a metaphor for God's curse:

> Thus says the LORD, "Behold, I am about to fill all the inhabitants of this land ... with drunkenness! And I will dash them against each other ... [and] destroy them." (Jer. 13:13-14)

> For thus says the Lord GOD, "Behold, I will give you into the hand of those whom you hate, into the hand of those from whom you were alienated. And they will deal with you in hatred, take all your property, and leave you naked and bare. And the nakedness of your harlotries shall be uncovered, both your lewdness and your harlotries. These things will be done to you because you have played the harlot with the nations, because you have defiled yourself with their idols. You have walked in the way of your sister; therefore I will give her cup into your hand."
> Thus says the Lord GOD,
> "You will drink your sister's cup,
> Which is deep and wide.
> You will be laughed at and held in derision;
> It contains much.
> You will be filled with drunkenness and sorrow,
> The cup of horror and desolation,
> The cup of your sister Samaria.
> And you will drink it and drain it.
> Then you will gnaw its fragments
> And tear your breasts;
> For I have spoken," declares the Lord GOD. (Ezek. 23:28-33)

Consequently, drunkenness leads inexorably to ruin and destruction, the very opposite condition of the blessing of God:

> For the heavy drinker and the glutton will come to poverty,
> And drowsiness will clothe a man with rags. (Prov. 23:21)

Whatever you devise against the LORD,
He will make a complete end of it.
Distress will not rise up twice.
Like tangled thorns,
And like those who are drunken with their drink,
They are consumed
As stubble completely withered. (Nah. 1:9-10)

Woe to you who make your neighbors drink,
Who mix in your venom even to make them drunk
So as to look on their nakedness!
You will be filled with disgrace rather than honor.
Now you yourself drink and expose your own nakedness.
The cup in the LORD's right hand will come around to you,
And utter disgrace will come upon your glory. (Hab. 2:15-16)

Rejoice and be glad, O daughter of Edom,
Who dwells in the land of Uz;
But the cup will come around to you as well,
You will become drunk and make yourself naked.
The punishment of your iniquity has been completed,
O daughter of Zion;
He will exile you no longer.
But He will punish your iniquity, O daughter of Edom;
He will expose your sins! (Lam. 4:21-22)

3. DISTORTS MAN'S PERCEPTION

The biblical worldview affirms the material world in which we live and avoids all gnostic escapism. The Christian interest in the material here-and-now should be evident in that: (1) God created the world and man's body as material entities, and all "very good" (Gen. 1:1-31; 2:7; Ps. 139:13-17). (2) Christ came in the flesh to redeem man from sin (Rom. 1:3; 9:5; Heb. 2:14-15; 1 John 4:1-3). (3) His Word directs us how to live in the present, material world (Mark 12:30; Rom. 12:1-2; 1 Cor. 6:13). (4) The believer's body is the temple of God (1 Cor. 3:16-17; 6:19; 2 Cor. 6:16). (5) God intends for us to remain on the earth for our fleshly sojourn, and does not remove us upon our being saved by his grace (Job 14:5; John 17:15; 2 Cor. 5:9-10). (6) Ultimately, the Lord equips us for the eternal new creation order by resurrecting us physically from the dead (John 5:28-29; Rom. 8:23; 1 Cor. 15).

As is obvious from these six observations, we have a genuine concern with the here-and-now. With this truth in mind, we must note that Scripture speaks of drunkenness as causing an illusory detachment from the real world that God has created:

> Who has woe? Who has sorrow?
> Who has contentions? Who has complaining?
> Who has wounds without cause?
> Who has redness of eyes?
> Those who linger long over wine,
> Those who go to taste mixed wine....
> Your eyes will see strange things,
> And your mind will utter perverse things. (Prov. 23:29-30, 33)

> And they shall drink and stagger and go mad because of the sword that I will send among them. (Jer. 25:16)

> And these also reel with wine and stagger from strong drink:
> The priest and the prophet reel with strong drink,
> They are confused by wine, they stagger from strong drink;
> They reel while having visions,
> They totter when rendering judgment. (Is. 28:7)

These passages explain why some in great sorrow and others who are miserable failures often pursue drink to the point of drunkenness. Alcohol serves as an escape mechanism that supposedly releases them from the burdens of their condition: "Harlotry, wine, and new wine take away the understanding" (Hos. 4:11). In fact, alcohol *can* be righteously used as a medicine for this very purpose:

Give strong drink to him who is perishing,
And wine to him whose life is bitter. (Prov. 31:6)

The escapist attempt to avoid one's problems is, of course, ultimately counterproductive, bringing more heaviness of heart: "Be on guard, that your hearts may not be weighted down with dissipation and drunkenness and the worries of life" (Luke 21:34). Again, as the Proverbs express the predicament of the drunkard: "Who has woe? Who has sorrow?" (Prov. 23:29)

4. DESTROYS VOCATIONAL CAPACITY

God places man in the world to exercise dominion in it (Gen. 1:26-28; 9:2-3; Ps. 8:5-8). Interestingly, at the very beginning of human history we see men engaging in cultural exploits well beyond the expectations of humanistic anthropologists and sociologists. Man's natural orientation to exercise dominion is actually a consequence of the image of God within (Gen. 1:26). Thus, even after sin enters the world, we find man subduing the earth and developing culture. He quickly develops various aspects of social culture: raising livestock, creating music, crafting tools, working with metal, and so forth (Gen. 4:20-22).

Upon his very creation, not only does God *call* man to develop all of creation, but man actually begins doing so.[1] Our cultural endeavors are not accidents of history, but consequences of God's creative will and calling (hence, the concept of "vocation," a term which comes from the Latin word for voice, *vox*).[2]

The Office of Prophet. The office of prophet is an important social institution in Old Testament Israel. Prophets are God's "lawyers" to prosecute the Lord's legal "case" (Hos. 4:1; Mic. 6:1) against Israel for breach of God's Law. Isaiah denounces the *prophet* who distorts God's message due to drunkenness:

> And these also reel with wine and stagger from strong drink:
> The priest and the prophet reel with strong drink,
> They are confused by wine, they stagger from strong drink;
> They reel while having visions,
> They totter when rendering judgment. (Is. 28:7)

Because of the enormous significance and benefit of the prophetic office, one aspect of God's judgment is cutting off prophecy from the land (Ps. 74:9; Is. 29:9). One way he does this is by plaguing Israel with incompetent prophets. Through Jeremiah God angrily threatens to fill the land with drunken prophets:

> Thus says the LORD, "Behold I am about to fill all the inhabitants of this land — the kings that sit for David on his throne, the priests, the prophets and all the inhabitants of Jerusalem — with drunkenness!" (Jer. 13:13)

The Office of Priest. Leviticus 10 enacts divine legislation for protecting the sacramental functions of the priesthood from abuse. After reading of Nadab and Abihu's offering of "strange fire" to the Lord (Lev. 10:1) and the Lord's lethal judgment upon them (Lev. 10:2), we hear God's word justifying his actions:

> Then Moses said to Aaron, "It is what the LORD spoke, saying,
> 'By those who come near Me I will be treated as holy,
> And before all the people I will be honored.'"
> So Aaron, therefore, kept silent. (Lev. 10:3)

Apparently before entering the sanctuary Nadab and Abihu had consumed enough wine to dull their judgment in conducting the worship of God. This appears so because of the prohibition immediately following:

> The LORD then spoke to Aaron, saying, "Do not drink wine or strong drink, neither you nor your sons with you, when you come into the tent of meeting, so that you may not die — it is a perpetual statute throughout your generations — and so as to make a distinction between the holy and the profane, and between the unclean and the clean, and so as to teach the sons of Israel all the statutes which the LORD has spoken to them through Moses." (Lev. 10:8-11)

The same sort of warning appears in Ezekiel 44:21: "Nor shall any of the priests drink wine when they enter the inner court."

The Office of King. In Proverbs one of the biblical directives regulating the office of king deals with alcohol consumption. Proverbs notes that *while engaging in the judicial affairs of state,* Scripture forbids kings from indulging in wine:

> It is not for kings, O Lemuel,
> It is not for kings to drink wine,
> Or for rulers to desire strong drink. (Prov. 31:4)

The Scripture immediately appends the rationale behind this prohibition:

> Lest they drink and forget what is decreed,
> and pervert the rights of the afflicted. (Prov. 31:5)

This same idea appears in a similar context, where Isaiah prophesies:

> Woe to those who are heroes in drinking wine,
> And valiant men in mixing strong drink;
> Who justify the wicked for a bribe,
> And take away the rights of the ones who are in the right!
> (Is. 5:22-23)

The Scripture records occasions of kings becoming drunk and causing political catastrophes: Elah (1 Kin. 16:9) and Ben-hadad (1 Kin. 20:16). It warns of drunkenness among the leadership of Ephraim (Is. 28:1, 3) and threatens drunkenness among the kings of Judah (Jer. 13:13) and of Babylon (Jer. 51:57). We also read of blessings upon kings not given to drunkenness: "Blessed are you, O land, whose king is of nobility and whose princes eat at the appropriate time — for strength, and not for drunkenness" (Eccl. 10:17). We should note that God does not send the blessing because of *abstinence*, but *sobriety*.

As an illustrative aside, in American history Thomas Jefferson laments alcohol addiction among political leaders:

> The habit of using ardent spirits by men in pubic office has often produced more injury to the public service, and more trouble to me, than any other circumstance that has occurred in the internal concerns of the country during my administration. And were I to commence my administration again, with the knowledge which from experience I have acquired, the first question that I would ask with regard to every candidate for office would be, "Is he addicted to the use of ardent spirits?"[3]

Clearly, wine has the capacity to dull one's analytical abilities thereby destroying one's vocational function — when indulged in immoderately. But we must not limit this predicament to political, prophetic, or ecclesiastical office. Solomon warns of the decline of one's productive output in any vocation:

> Do not be with heavy drinkers of wine,
> Or with gluttonous eaters of meat;
> For the heavy drinker and the glutton will come to poverty,
> And drowsiness will clothe a man with rags. (Prov. 23:20)

5. IS SOCIALLY DISGUSTING

Scripture commands Christians to live circumspect lives (Eph. 5:15-16). We are to live in such a manner that we will bring glory to God (Matt. 5:16; 1 Cor. 6:20; 1 Pet. 4:16), not being a cause for rebuke (2 Cor. 8:21; Phil. 2:15; Titus 2:8; 1 Pet. 2:12-21).

Contrary to such obligations, drunkenness causes men to breach standards of social decorum: "And these also reel with wine and stagger from strong drink: The priest and the prophet reel with strong drink, they are confused by wine, they stagger from strong drink; they reel while having visions, they totter when rendering judgment. For all the tables are full of filthy vomit, without a single clean place" (Is. 28:7-8). A turn through the pages of Scripture reveals other such examples:

> Thus says the LORD of hosts, the God of Israel, "Drink, be drunk, vomit, fall, and rise no more." (Jer. 25:27)

> They reeled and staggered like a drunken man. (Ps. 107:27)

> They grope in darkness with no light
> And He makes them stagger like a drunken man. (Job 12:25)

Not only is the drunkard's conduct disorderly and repulsive, but he acts contentiously, making him socially obnoxious: "Who has contentions? Who has complaining? … Those who linger long over wine…. Your mind will utter perverse things" (Prov. 23:29-30, 33). Another similar example is found in Habakkuk:

> You will be filled with disgrace rather than honor.
> Now you yourself drink and expose your own nakedness.
> The cup in the LORD's right hand will come around to you,
> And utter disgrace will come upon your glory. (2:16)

Thus, drunkenness becomes a metaphor for violence:

> For they eat the bread of wickedness,
> And drink the wine of violence.
> (Prov. 4:17)

> Wine is a mocker, strong drink a brawler,
> And whoever is intoxicated by it is not wise. (Prov. 20:1)

Here in Proverbs 20:1, using metonymy[†] the writer substitutes "wine" for the drunkard himself. That is, "mocker" and "brawler" actually refer to the drunkard.

6. WEAKENS THE BODY

Man's body is God's handiwork (Gen. 2:7; 1 Cor. 12:24). As such it should inspire our awe of God's marvelous creative power and glorious wisdom (Ps. 139:13-15; Job 10:8-12; Eccl. 11:5). As Christians we should strive to maintain healthy bodies, for the body is the temple of the Holy Spirit (1 Cor. 3:16-17; 6:19-20; 2 Cor. 6:16) wherein we serve God (Rom. 12:1; 1 Cor. 9:27).

† Metonymy is a rhetorical device in which the name of one thing is switched with another because the two are readily associated — one implying the other. "A common example," notes A. Berkeley Mickelsen, "is the use of 'the White House' to refer to the President, e.g., 'The White House decided to release the speech earlier than usual.'" See: Mickelsen, 185-186.

To "linger long at the wine," however, is physically dangerous because at the last "it bites like a serpent" and "stings like a viper" (Prov. 23:30, 32). Thus, overindulging can lead to becoming "sick with the heat of wine" (Hos. 7:5). Indeed, often "a drunken man staggers in his vomit" (Is. 5:22-23; 19:14; 28:7; 56:12), being nauseated.

While the nature of alcohol is not my foremost concern in this study, nevertheless, we should keep in mind that overindulgence in alcohol does result in serious, debilitating, physiological harm to the alcoholic. Although medically it seems that alcohol itself "does not cause any known damage to the body,"[4] however, the *manner* and *quantity* of alcohol consumed can and does indirectly cause various ailments.[5] Thus, chronic alcoholism (as both Scripture and experience teach) destroys one's physical well-being. In contrast to such dangers in alcohol abuse, God obligates Christians to nourish and cherish their bodies (Eph. 5:29). God desires our good health (1 Tim. 5:23; James 5:14-15; 3 John 2), and as a matter of fact, many of the case laws of the Old Testament were concerned with health and sanitation for fostering bodily strength (Lev. 13:46; Deut. 20:12-13).[6]

7. CORRUPTS MORALS

With excessive alcohol ingestion, moral sensitivity diminishes. In fact, abuse of wine dulls one's perceptiveness and ability to properly interact with his environment. Thus, God mocks the dullness of the heavy drinker who does not see the calamity coming his way:

> "Come," they say, "let us get wine, and let us drink heavily of strong drink;
> And tomorrow will be like today, only more so." (Is. 56:12)

The classic illustration of the moral impact of drunkenness is history's first recorded episode. Of Noah we read, "And he drank of the wine and became drunk, and uncovered himself inside his tent" (Gen. 9:21).

In another episode the daughters of Lot connive to wash away their father's moral restraints by use of wine: "Come, let us make our father drink wine, and let us lie with him, that we may preserve our family through our father" (Gen. 19:32). Their plan was as successful as it was evil.

Such potential immorality among the drunken later becomes material for prophetic curse:

> You will become drunk and make yourself naked. (Lam. 4:21)

> They have also cast lots for My people,
> Traded a boy for a harlot,
> And sold a girl for wine that they may drink. (Joel 3:3)

Consequently, it is not surprising that overindulgence in wine causes spiritual indifference, as illustrated in Isaiah 5:11-12:

> Woe to those who rise early in the morning that they may pursue strong drink;
> Who stay up late in the evening that wine may inflame them!
> And their banquets are accompanied by lyre and harp, by tambourine and flute, and by wine;
> But they do not pay attention to the deeds of the LORD,
> Nor do they consider the work of His hands.

Numerous references press home the point of moral turpitude among the abusers of alcoholic beverage. Already quoted was Proverbs 20:1: "Wine is a mocker, strong drink a brawler, and whoever is intoxicated by it is not wise." Other examples:

> Furthermore, wine betrays the haughty man,
> So that he does not stay at home.
> He enlarges his appetite like Sheol,
> And he is like death, never satisfied. (Hab. 2:5)

> Instead, there is gaiety and gladness,
> Killing of cattle and slaughtering of sheep,
> Eating of meat and drinking of wine:
> "Let us eat and drink, for tomorrow we may die." (Is. 22:13)

> Harlotry, wine, and new wine take away the understanding. (Hos. 4:11).

Thus, too, Scripture frequently includes drunkenness in verses relating a complex of immoral vices inimical to Christian conduct: "Let us behave properly as in the day, not in carousing and drunkenness, not in sexual promiscuity and sensuality, not in strife and jealousy" (Rom. 13:13).

From Galatians, Chapter 5: "Now the deeds of the flesh are evident, which are: immorality, impurity, sensuality, idolatry, sorcery, enmities, strife, jealousy, outbursts of anger, disputes, dissensions, factions, envying, drunkenness, carousing, and things like these, of which I forewarn you just as I have forewarned you that those who practice such things shall not inherit the kingdom of God" (vv. 19-21).

And from 1 Peter, Chapter 4: "For the time already past is sufficient for you to have carried out the desire of the Gentiles, having pursued a course of sensuality, lusts, drunkenness, carousals, drinking parties and abominable idolatries. And in all this, they are surprised that you do not run with them into the same excess of dissipation, and they malign you" (vv. 3-4).

8. BARS FROM CHURCH LEADERSHIP

Paul provides us with much instruction regarding church leadership. He also warns of various ecclesiastical repercussions several times in his pastoral letters. In those letters he outlines prerequisites for both ordained ecclesiastical office and other forms of church service. Several of these involve his denunciation of wine *abuse*:

> An overseer, then, must be not addicted to wine. (1 Tim. 3:2-3)

> Deacons likewise must be men of dignity, not double-tongued, or addicted to much wine. (1 Tim. 3:8)

Older women likewise are to be reverent in their behavior, not malicious gossips, not enslaved to much wine. (Titus 2:3)

This restriction is made not only because drunkenness is itself a heinous sin (points 1, 2, and 7 above). Nor is it due only to the necessity of church leaders possessing clarity of thought in order to properly "think God's thoughts after Him" (points 3, 4, and 8). But it arises also because the leader must to be an example to the church (1 Cor. 11:1; Phil. 3:17; 2 Thess. 3:7-9; 1 Tim. 4:12; Heb. 6:12; 13:7, 17) and to the world (Matt. 10:16; 1 Tim. 3:7; 2 Tim. 2:24-26; Titus 2:7-8), living a life of godliness.

Reynolds objects to the moderationist treatment of these passages: "To forbid much does not permit a little. Such a prohibition merely fails to speak of moderation."[7] But this seems a rather weak rebuttal. If the Scripture is warning of alcohol consumption, why does it not *clearly* forbid *all* wine? Why do we have commands that forbid "addiction" and "much wine"? Reynolds' attempt to dull the force of these statements simply will not suffice.

Van Impe muses over such texts as these, noting that Paul "does not open the door in this text to *some* wine anymore than to *some* gossip or *some* greed."[8] But this *assumes* what needs to be proved: that partaking of wine is *itself* sin. Also note that Scripture does not merely prohibit "*much* gossip" or "*much* greed." It condemns gossip and greed outright, whereas it does nothing of the sort regarding wine.

CONCLUSION

The biblical data is clear in denouncing all forms of alcohol abuse (whether occasional over-indulgence, binge drunkenness, or chronic drunkenness). With unmistakable emphasis, the Scriptures condemn drunkenness on physiological and social grounds, as well as for spiritual and moral reasons. God vigorously denounces those who "linger long at the wine" (Prov. 23:30), who are "given to much wine" (1 Tim. 3:8), who "rise early in the morning that they may pursue drink" (Is. 5:11).

Having noted these important matters, we must be careful, however, to avoid wrongly equating *drunkenness* with *drinking*. To condemn *all* use of alcoholic beverage — including moderate, sacramental, and medicinal uses — by resorting to scriptural prohibitions against *drunkenness* would be to engage in fallacious ethical reasoning. Perhaps the error of such reasoning can best be illustrated syllogistically, as follows:

1. Scripture condemns drunkenness	1. Scripture condemns gluttony	1. Scripture condemns infidelity
2. Drinking alcohol can lead to drunkness	2. Enjoying food can lead to gluttony	2. Enjoying sex can lead to sexual infidelity
3. Therefore, Scripture condemns all alcohol drinking	3. Therefore, Scripture condemns all food consumption	3. Therefore, Scripture condemns all sexual activity

Looking at the matter in this way, just because Scripture condemns drunkenness (the *abuse* of alcohol), it does not necessarily follow that it also condemns moderate, occasional, and temperate drinking of alcoholic beverages (a *use* of alcohol). Although Scripture frequently parallels gluttony with drunkenness (Deut. 21:20; Prov. 23:21; Matt. 11:19; Luke 7:34), surely all eating is not condemned! Though the Bible often associates sexual infidelity and drunkenness (Rom. 13:13; 1 Pet. 4:3; Rev. 17:2), who would condemn all sexual activity?

Consequently, our investigating the matter of the Christian, the Bible, and alcohol must continue further.

CHAPTER 3
THE OLD TESTAMENT AND ALCOHOL USE

In the preceding chapter I show the various ways in which Scripture *condemns* alcohol abuse. The moderationist agrees with the prohibitionist and abstentionist in standing against such immoderate behavior. But now we must consider the direct question whether Scripture allows *any* consumption of alcoholic beverage.

To properly understand the scriptural pronouncements on alcohol consumption, we must engage in a lexical analysis of the various Hebrew and Greek words most prominently employed to refer to alcoholic drink in the Bible. Although numerous Hebrew terms appear in the Old Testament, our study will concentrate on four particularly significant words: *yayin*, *shekar*, *tirosh*, and *'asis*. In the New Testament, two Greek words require our attention: *oinos* and *gleukos*. In this chapter, I will focus on the Old Testament material; in the next chapter the New Testament.

THE HEBREW TERM *YAYIN*

By far the most common and therefore most important word for "wine" in the Old Testament is *yayin*, which occurs in the Hebrew text 141 times. Consequently, I will spend more time establishing the meaning of this term than the meanings of the other three.

According to lexical scholars *yayin* is apparently a word borrowed from another language, and its root meaning is somewhat obscure.[1] Yet lexicographers agree *yayin* is functionally equivalent to the Greek term *oinos* and the Latin *vinum*.[2] The evidence clearly shows that *yayin* is a fermented beverage derived from grapes. Please note the following ninefold argument for the intoxicating capacity of *yayin*, demonstrating its alcoholic nature.

1. LEXICAL CONSENSUS

The various Hebrew lexicons and Old Testament dictionaries and encyclopedias agree that *yayin* is a fermented beverage, not simply grape juice. Consider the following few samples:

The Brown-Driver-Briggs lexicon offers a simple and unambiguous meaning for *yayin*: It lists as its meaning the English word "wine," noting that it is "intoxicating."[3]

In an article published in the *Theological Wordbook of the Old Testament* (and written by Old Testament scholar and strict abstentionist R. Laird Harris), we read that "its intoxicating properties are mentioned at least twenty times." He continues: "Wine was the most intoxicating drink known in ancient times."[4]

Strong's Concordance states simply of *yayin* that it is "from an unused root mean[ing] to *effervesce*; *wine* (as fermented); by impl[ication] *intoxication*."[5] Davidson's *Analytical Hebrew and Chaldee Lexicon* defines the term very simply: "Root not used; to which is ascribed the signification of *heat and fermentation*.... I. *wine*. — II. meton[ymy for] *intoxication*."[6]

Interestingly, prohibitionist advocate and Semitic languages scholar Stephen M. Reynolds admits that "the Talmud gives support to the idea that it was regarded as an intoxicant in post-biblical (but nevertheless ancient) Hebrew.

Thus in *Yoma* 76b ... we read: 'Why is it (wine) called *"yayin"* and *"tirosh"*? It is called *"yayin"* because it brings lamentation into the world, and *"tirosh"* because he who indulges in it becomes poor.'"[7] Thus, ancient Hebrews speaking their *own language* affirm *yayin's* fermented quality — as even one of the most vigorous opponents of this view admits.

Prohibitionists often note this unanimity and decry it. For instance, Wilkerson laments, "I have searched out the old Bible commentaries and almost all of them suggest wine referred to in the Old and New Testaments was fermented."[8] Teachout does the same : "Unfortunately Bible scholars have been equally misled by public opinion."[9] But when you search out all the scholars and find them unanimously differing with your opinion, who is really mistaken?

This "problem" is so frustrating to prohibitionists that they often defy the authorities and generate unique positions. Reynolds — a Hebrew scholar of note, and a member of the Old Testament translation committee of the *New International Version* — relentlessly maneuvers around the lexical evidence. Consider the following excerpts from his book, *The Biblical Approach to Alcohol*:

> God does not provide us with an inerrant dictionary of the ancient languages. (p. 9)

> God has never provided that translators should be inerrant. (p. 17)

> What follows is as far as I know an innovation. (p. 35)

> We must not rely even on generally accepted English dictionaries in determining what a word may or may not mean when used by educated speakers of the English language. Dictionary writers are bound up in their prejudices, a common human failing. (p. 139)

Of his own view he writes, "The improbable must be the correct answer. That is, the hypothesis that *shemarim* in Isaiah 25:6† does not mean *lees* at all. It is true that the lexicographers do not recognize any other meaning for *shemer* than dregs, lees or sediment, but we must face the improbable answer that they are incorrect in this particular verse" (p. 60).

† Isaiah 25:6: "The LORD of Hosts will prepare a lavish banquet for all the peoples on this mountain; a banquet of aged wines...." What the *New American Standard* renders "aged wine" is elsewhere translated "wine on the lees," referring to wine that has been allowed to fully ferment and mature.

To affirm his view, that "wine on the lees" does not actually mean "wine aged to full maturity," he resorts to criticizing the *New International Version* (p. 62) and disagreeing with the 1985 Jewish translation of the Hebrew Old Testament (Tanakh), which he lauded as, "Accomplished by Jewish scholars judged by competent Jewish people to be extremely well qualified to bring the Hebrew Scriptures to the large and generally well-educated world of English speaking adherents of Judaism" (p. 63).

Regarding his interpretation of other references to lees (or "dregs," as in Psalms 75:8), he admits, "I know of no previous writer who has suggested it" (p. 75). Elsewhere he confesses, "It is true that this translation may appear somewhat innovative" (p. 78).

2. TRANSLATIONAL AGREEMENT

We may rest assured that *yayin* is the fermented product of the grape and has the ability to intoxicate by noting how *all* modern Bible translation committees handle the term. They invariably translate it as "wine," rather than "juice," "must," "drink," or some other such non-alcoholic term.

Interestingly, Reynolds, a translator of the *New International Version*, argues, "There is a word *must* which could be used.... This by definition would be a good word to substitute for wine when the sense of Scripture demands it."[10] Yet, *no reputable translation does so*. Those who insist that intoxication was not necessarily within the capacity of *yayin* are set against well-established lexical authorities working in consensus on these translations. Consult any noted contemporary version of Scripture to verify this.

In addition, Numbers 6:3 uses the phrase *mishrath-enabiem*, translated "grape juice" in most versions of the Bible.† Why is *this* phrase not used to distinguish non-alcoholic beverage throughout the Old Testament?

† See, for instance, the *New American Standard Bible, King James Version, New Revised Standard Version*, and Reynolds' own *NIV*.

The *New Bible Dictionary* provides an insightful comment bolstering this point: "While there are examples of the grapes being pressed into a cup and presumably used at once (Gen. 40:11), it is significant that the term 'wine' is never applied to the resultant grape juice."[11] Genesis 40:11 reads, "Now Pharaoh's cup was in my hand; so I took the grapes and squeezed them into Pharaoh's cup, and I put the cup into Pharaoh's hand."

3. FIRST MENTION

J. D. Davis points out that *yayin* must be an intoxicant, due to the interpretive principle of *first mention*: "When the Hebrew word *yayin* first occurs in Scripture, it is the fermented juice of the grape (Gen. 9:21), and there is no reason to believe that it has a different meaning elsewhere."[12] In other words, the very first time we come upon this word in Scripture, we see it intoxicating Noah. It certainly is not simple grape juice. The "argument from first mention" requires that later changes in the denotation of the term should be clearly presented — but none are.

4. CONTEXTUAL USAGE

Numerous Old Testament passages mention the intoxicating capacity of *yayin*, thereby indicating its fermented quality. For instance, the Scripture casually alludes to cases of drunkenness caused by *yayin*, as if it is not surprising that anyone could be intoxicated by it: Noah (Gen. 9:21), Lot (Gen. 19:32-35), Nabal (1 Sam. 25:36-37), Uriah (2 Sam. 11:13), Elah (1 Kin. 16:9), Ben-hadad (1 Kin. 20:16), Ahasuerus (Esth. 1:10-11), Belshazzar (Dan. 5:1-6), and the "proud of Ephraim" (Is. 28:1), to name but a few. These are examples of men who become tragically drunk and morally degraded by consuming too much *yayin*.

As I note in Chapter 2, *inordinate* consumption of *yayin* can lead to lax morals (Prov. 23:33; Hab. 2:5), invariably overcomes sound judgment (Prov. 23:35; Is. 56:12), serves as a symbol of God's wrath (Ps. 60:3; 75:8; Jer. 25:15-17) — and more. Solomon even deems *yayin* "a mocker" (Prov. 20:1). Prohibitionist Reynolds comments on *yayin* in Habakkuk 2:5, "The evil that alcohol can do is here exhibited in all its ugliness."[13] He even notes that here "God calls us to contemplate the evils of drunkenness."[14] Surely these effects and uses cannot refer to mere grape juice.

Fundamentalist Old Testament scholar Merrill F. Unger observes that "in most of the passages in the Bible where *yayin* is used… it certainly means fermented grape juice, and in the remainder it may be fairly presumed to do so. In no passage can it be positively shown to have any other meaning. The intoxicating character of *yayin* in general is plain from Scripture."[15]

In a study strongly discouraging alcohol consumption, abstentionist Old Testament scholar R. L. Harris comments that *yayin* means "wine" and "is frequently condemned, often associated with drunkenness, and seldom spoken of in any favorable light."[16] In fact, he writes, "almost half of the passages mentioning *yayin* in the Old Testament are clearly denunciatory."[17] Obviously, then, *yayin* possesses inebriating qualities.

5. WINE PRODUCTION

When we consider the (admittedly scant) biblical references to wine production, we discover that Israelites *intentionally* prepare the grape juice in a way that intensifies and enhances the fermentation process. Three passages allude to this practice: Isaiah 25:6, Jeremiah 48:11, and Zephaniah 1:12. Since the latter two are entirely metaphorical, however, we will look only at the first passage.

In the *King James Version,* Isaiah 25:6 reads, "And in this mountain shall the LORD of hosts make unto all people a feast of fat things, a feast of wines on the lees, of fat things full of marrow, of wines on the lees well refined." The *New American Standard*, recall, renders this "aged wine."

E. J. Young comments on the passage, "By means of gradation, Isaiah now characterizes the banquet as one of wine that is matured by resting undisturbed on the lees. A play upon words as well as a gradation appears between *shemanim* (fat things) and *shemarim* (lees). This latter word originally signified holders or preservers and then came to designate the wines that had rested a long time on sediment or dregs, and so had become more valuable. The wine lay on the lees to increase its strength and color."[18]

Tregelles agrees with this assessment in his revision of Gesenius' Hebrew lexicon: "*shemarim*, m. dregs (of wine) so called because, when wine is kept on the lees, its strength and color are preserved."[19]

This becomes all the more remarkable in that prohibitionists — such as Reynolds, Patton, Wilkerson, and

Teachout — are fond of noting the ancients could retard the fermentation process.[20] They often cite comments by Virgil (*Georgics* 1:295), Pliny (*Natural History* 14:11:83), Columella (*On Agriculture* 12:29:1), Cato (*On Agriculture* 120:1), and others. We are compelled to ask, then, why does the Bible itself never encourage or even *mention* such processes? Especially if — as per the prohibitionist — it condemns alcoholic beverages? Their pointing to (alleged) ancient fermentation preventative technology actually strengthens the moderationist argument.

† For a helpful discussion of the processes of aerobic and anaerobic fermentation, and ancient storage practices, see Bustanoby, Chapter 3.

I should point out, though, that the various instructions from the ancients do not prevent fermentation. For instance, stoppering bottles of grape juice actually begins the process of *anaerobic* fermentation which promotes fermentation in the absence of free air. Adding sulfur kills the bacteria that causes the *degrading* of wine into vinegar.†

6. LIMITED RESTRICTIONS

That *yayin* is alcoholic also appears from its occasional prohibition to priests and kings. Here the reader should recall my previous discussion about how drunkenness destroys vocational capacity (Chapter 2). There I note that one of the biblical directives regulating the office of king prohibits his consuming *yayin* while engaging in the affairs of state, lest he diminish his perception:

> It is not for kings, O Lemuel,
> It is not for kings to drink wine,
> Or for rulers to desire strong drink.
> Lest they drink and forget what is decreed,
> And pervert the rights of the afflicted. (Prov. 31:4-5)

We may make the same observation in God's prohibiting priests from partaking of *yayin* when engaging in sacerdotal functions. Immediately after God destroys Nadab and Abihu for offering "strange fire" which he had not commanded, he warns Aaron, "The LORD then spoke to Aaron, saying, 'Do not drink wine or strong drink, neither you nor your sons with you, *when you come into the tent of meeting*, so that you may not die — it is a perpetual statute throughout your generations — and so as to make a distinction between the holy and the profane, and between the unclean and the clean'" (Lev. 10:8-10). Ezekiel 44:21 reflects the same concern: "Nor shall any of the priests drink wine *when they enter the inner court*." Josephus mentions this as continuing for this reason in his day: "The priests abide therein both nights and days, performing certain purifications, and drinking not the least drop of wine *while they are in the temple*" (*Apion* 1:22).

Thus, we see that God warns men in *certain circumstances* and on *specific occasions* to forgo *yayin* consumption. Clearly these directives *assume* the inebriating potential of *yayin*. Interestingly, this fermented *yayin* is not *absolutely* prohibited — God forbids it only on certain occasions. Why does he not condemn it altogether, rather than just in defined and limited circumstances?

7. FAILED ALTERNATIVES

Many prohibitionists argue that there were two types of *yayin* — one fermented and the other unfermented. For instance, Reynolds, a translator of the *New International Version* and an able proponent of prohibition, comments:

> *Yayin* is assumed by many people to be always an alcoholic drink. This is a mistake which has led to much confusion and to much intoxication which might easily have been avoided. Isaiah 16:10 says: "No treader shall tread out *yayin*

in the presses." This obviously means that no treader shall tread out grape juice in the presses, because fermentation is a time consuming process. Therefore alcohol is excluded from the word *yayin* in this passage.[21]

He then immediately adds, "This is enough to establish the fact that *yayin* in the Bible need not be alcoholic." Elsewhere, he vigorously presses the point of Isaiah 16:10: "it would be absurd to translate *yayin* as *fermented grape juice*."[22]

Yet, in the *International Standard Bible Encyclopedia*, C. M. Kerr states categorically that "to insist on a distinction between intoxicating and unfermented wine is a case of unjustified special pleading."[23] Unger agrees: "Some, indeed, have argued from these passages [i.e., passages speaking favorably of *yayin*] that *yayin* could not always have been alcoholic. But this is begging the question, and that in defiance of the facts."[24]

Despite the prima facie plausibility of Reynolds' argument, however, a closer analysis of Isaiah 16:10 demonstrates his point lacks merit. Indeed, his argument is not only exegetically flawed but undercut by other statements and principles contained elsewhere in his own book. Exegetically we should note that the verse in question appears in a poetic context. The poetic license so common in Hebrew poetry will allow the freshly expressed *yayin* here to be alcoholic, just as it may speak of wine itself as being a "brawler" (rather than the one who actually drinks the wine, Prov. 20:1).

A common literary device is *prolepsis*. Prolepsis is the anachronistic representing of something as existing *before* its proper or historical time. Prolepsis looks to the *end result* anticipated in the proleptic observation. The Scripture is filled with examples of prolepsis, several of which directly parallel Isaiah 16:10. For instance, in Judges 9:13 "wine"

(Heb. *tirosh*, a liquid drink processed from grapes) is spoken of as on the "vine," just as figs exist on the tree (Judg. 9:10-12). But, of course, *grapes* appear as a solid fruit on the vine — though *tirosh* is the ultimate liquid drink produced from the grapes. In Isaiah 65:8 we find "new wine" (Heb. *tirosh*) "in the cluster." Jeremiah 40:10 speaks of "gathering in wine" (Heb. *tirosh*) as if the liquid drink itself were in the field on the vine. The Old Testament has a word for grapes, as literal fruit on the vine: *enab* (Gen. 40:10-11; Lev. 25:5; Num. 6:3-4). Rather than use *enab*, however, the Old Testament writers chose the poetic, figurative use of the word *tirosh* in these passages.

Clearly then, Reynolds errs in arguing as he does from Isaiah 16:10. The error is serious enough in that he emphasizes it as "enough to establish the fact" (which it does not) — but then he employs it again a few pages later (p. 28) as an assured conclusion.

In addition, Reynolds compounds his error when later in the same book he makes observations that in principle undermine his own case. For instance, on page 25 of *The Biblical Approach to Alcohol* he refers to *tirosh*, which is another word for "wine" — or, given his argument, "grape juice." There he notes that "reference to its being found in the cluster (Is. 65:8) and to its suffering in time of drought (Is. 24:7) are understood to be poetical" (p. 25). Precisely! And just as biblical writers can say that *tirosh* (a liquid product) is found in "cluster" (the solid fruit, Is. 65:8), so can they declare that *yayin* (fermented wine) is "treaded out" from grapes (Is. 16:10). Obviously, *tirosh* is in the cluster in that it is the *product* to be derived from the grape.

Interestingly, Reynolds argues by a very similar method (i.e., proleptic statement) when explaining Ephesians 5:18:

† Reynolds, *Alcohol*, 53.
Please note that I believe
Reynolds is mistaken in
this observation (as I will
next argue). My point is to
show dialectical tension in
Reynolds' argument.

Some commentators say that the words
"in which" refer to the whole phrase,
"Be not drunk with wine," and not just
to "wine." The wish not to accept the
idea that debauchery is "in" wine
makes them reject this obvious sense,
and choose instead the idea that it lies
in being drunk. But end results are
sometimes attributed to the substance
which causes the results.†

Reynolds even defines *prolepsis* for us: "Prolepsis (which may also be called anticipation) is the treating of a future event as though it had already happened, or the giving of a name to something as though it existed before it came to be."[25]

We should note that if the principle of "end results" (i.e., prolepsis or "anticipation") is legitimate in the *prose* of Ephesians 5, it should be equally appropriate in the *poetry* of Isaiah 16:10 — especially since poetry, by its very nature, allows liberty in expression. Thus, based on Reynolds' own argument, we can say that *fermented* wine is "treaded out in the presses," because "end results are sometimes attributed to the substance which causes the result." Clearly then, the critical argument put forward by Reynolds is not established at all.

Dunlop Moore was not impressed by such "two-wine" maneuvers in his day, when they first arose: "In fact, the theory of two kinds of wine — the one fermented and intoxicating and unlawful, and the other unfermented, unintoxicating, and lawful — is a modern hypothesis, devised during the present century, and has no foundation in the Bible, or in Hebrew or classical antiquity."[26]

Interestingly, in Reynolds' later work, *The Biblical Approach to Alcohol* — wherein he specifically defends his views against my earlier critique of them† — he includes an appendix written by my ministerial friend Robert E. Baxter who accuses me of circular reasoning: "Mr. Gentry argues in circles. The reasoning goes like this: 'Wine' in the Bible is always fermented. When the Bible speaks negatively of wine, it is referring to the ABUSE of wine, not its USE."[27] But is it circular reasoning to argue that when Mr. X sips one glass of wine and does not get drunk, he merely *uses* it, but when Mr. Y guzzles fifteen glasses of wine and gets drunk, he *abuses* it? Where is the circle? This is no more circular than saying, "Mr. A *used* a gun by firing it at a target on the firing range, while Mr. B *abused* a gun by firing it at a three-year-old child across the street." Likewise, it is not circular to note that those who "linger long over the wine" (Prov. 23:30; 1 Tim. 3:8; Titus 2:3) are *abusing* wine, while those who partake in moderation are simply *using* wine in a tolerable way. My argument simply draws necessary moral distinctions between use and abuse.

What is worse, the two-wine theory promoted by both Baxter and Reynolds follows the precise pattern of reasoning condemned by Baxter in Reynolds' own book! Reynolds argues that "favorable references to *oinos* [the New Testament word for *wine*] mean the unfermented kind, and unfavorable ones the fermented."[28] This form of argument appears repeatedly in *The Biblical Approach to Alcohol*.[29] In fact, this is virtually a universal practice throughout the prohibitionist literature. Consider the following samples:

Moses Stuart: "When the Scriptures speak of wine as a comfort, a blessing, or a libation to God ... they can mean

† Reynolds' second book specifically interacts with my earlier work no less than a dozen times (though most of the times he does not mention my name — although he directly engages my exact arguments). Reynolds and I have also held a published debate in *Antithesis* 2:2 (March/April 1991), 41-49.

only such wine as contained no alcohol that could have mischievous tendency; that wherever they denounce it and connect it with drunkenness and revelry, they can mean only alcoholic or intoxicating wine."[30]

William Patton: "The careful reader of the Bible will have noticed that in a number of cases wine is simply mentioned, without anything in the context to determine its character. He will have noticed another class, which unmistakably denotes the bad character of the beverage. He will also have noticed a third class, whose character is as clearly designated as good.... Can it be that these blessings and curses refer to the same beverage, and that an intoxicating liquor? Does the trumpet give a certain or an uncertain sound?"[31]

Robert Teachout: "The implied fermentation or its lack [is] to be determined objectively only from the divine approval or disapproval of the beverage indicated by any context."[32]

Jack Van Impe: He not only favorably quotes Teachout's statement, but provides an appendix titled, "Correct Uses of the Hebrew Words Translated 'Wine' in the *King James Version* Bible (in the Judgment of the Authors)."[33] In that appendix he lists each occurrence of "wine" in the *King James Version* and states whether he believes it is fermented or unfermented based solely on whether the references are favorable or not.

The approach shared by these prohibitionist proponents is a genuinely question-begging argument. It begins the moral inquiry into Scripture with the very assumption that must be proved. Interestingly, several scriptures mention wine in a good sense and a bad sense in the *same* contexts: 1 Samuel 1:14, 24; 25:18, 37; and Joel 1:5, 10. The product is the same; the employment of the product differs.

8. QUALIFIED SILENCE

Interestingly, the Scripture itself never draws a distinction between "safe" and "unsafe" *yayin* — as if the "problem" is in a certain kind of wine, rather than in the volume consumed or the person recklessly partaking. That is, the Bible never commands us to avoid alcoholic *yayin* while encouraging us to consume only the non-alcoholic product of the grape. Though this is an argument from silence, it is one of those valuable instances where "silence is golden." If the Scripture resolutely condemns drunkenness and alcohol dependence, why does it not demarcate safe and unsafe *yayin* — especially since prohibitionists emphatically inform us that two types of *yayin* exist? Why do we not find in the detailed legislation of Exodus, Leviticus, or Deuteronomy, for instance, any condemnation of producing or consuming *fermented* wine? The Mosaic legislation imposes many moral injunctions upon Israel, but never one prohibiting the partaking of alcoholic beverages — though it *does* condemn drunkenness (Deut. 21:20).

This becomes so glaring a problem — or should I say, so deafening a silence — for prohibitionists that Reynolds offers a desperate response to it: God "left a number of things somewhat difficult to perceive as a test of the spiritual perception of Bible readers,"[34] stating elsewhere that "in the same way God may have left His true teaching concerning alcoholic beverages with what the undiscerning find to be ambiguities."[35]

In his defense of prohibitionism, in fact, he frequently employs biblical "paradoxes,"[†] "ambiguities,"[36] and "enigmas"[37] as a *deus ex machina* to save his prohibitionist system.

† Reynolds, *Alcohol*, 8-10. Giving himself an "escape route" from the clear word of Scripture, Reynolds begins his study of the issue before us with these words: "There are paradoxes in the Bible about a number of matters" (p. 8).

Indeed, in the opinion of Reynolds, "God may place these enigmas in the Bible here and there to make believers search diligently.... In the same way He may have left the teaching concerning the command to total abstinence somewhat obscure as a test to determine who among those who profess to believe in Him would discern His true meaning."[38] But then again, maybe he did not. Maybe God meant what he said!

Reynolds continues this line of argument and defense in his larger, follow-up work, *The Biblical Approach to Alcohol*. The very first two sentences in his first chapter of this work read, "There are paradoxes in the Bible about a number of matters. One paradox which has caused great disharmony among Christians is the contradictory statements about what are thought to be alcoholic drinks."[39] Later he queries, "If anyone should ask, why did God not make the prohibition of alcoholic beverages for pleasure so clear in all parts of the Bible, that everyone, no matter what his stage of spiritual development, can understand, the answer is, He is under no obligation to do that."[40]

This becomes all the more troublesome when we note that Reynolds *himself* suggests two other Hebrew terms that he believes refer to alcoholic beverages:

1. *Ki yith'addam*. Reynolds' favorite biblical statement for his prohibitionist views is Proverbs 23:31, which reads, "Do not look on the wine *when it is red*."[41] Of the key phrase here, he argues, "The meaning 'when it is alcoholic' for *ki yith'addam* may have become obsolete in common Hebrew" in the time of the translation of the Septuagint.[42] But he insists it was the original meaning. In fact, he vigorously argues for the phrase meaning "it is alcoholic," in that *redness* is a common descriptor for alcoholic drinks, such as "red-eye" or "red-nose." This is due to redness indicating the

"blood-shot eyes of drinkers, or *red-nose*, referring to their noses."[43]

2. *Chemer.* Reynolds comments on Psalm 75:8, which references foaming wine, "It is therefore proposed that *chamar* in Psalm 75:9 [or verse 8, depending on translation] means *it is alcoholic.*" Later he writes, "It is now the time to give evidence that the noun *chemer*, from the same root as the verb *chamar*, means *alcoholic drink* and in connection with the expression 'blood of the grape,' it means *alcoholic wine.*"[44] He vigorously asserts, "*chamar* signifies neither *it is red* nor *it is foaming* but *it is alcoholic.*"[45] He translates Deuteronomy 32:14, "the blood of the grape thou shalt drink — alcoholic wine."[46] The Hebrew phrase is *wedham — 'enab tishteh chamer.* Reynolds notes that the translation "fiery wine" here is acceptable, in that it "refers to the heat caused by the alcohol as it goes into the mouth and throat."†

Strangely enough, Reynolds (to my surprise) claims that the speakers of biblical Hebrew "probably used *yayin mi-gat* or something similar, meaning unfermented wine, and *yayin ki yith' addam*, or *chemer* when it was necessary to say without fear of misunderstanding that they were speaking of intoxicating wine."[47] He even comments on Sanhedrin 70a that "Newly pressed wine, prior to fermentation, was known as *yayin mi-gat* (wine from the press)."[48] Why then does Scripture not *commonly* employ these words to distinguish *alcoholic* wine that God forbids from non-alcoholic wine that God allows? Had God intended us to avoid alcoholic wine, he could have made the matter clear in Scripture. But he does not. The phraseology

† Reynolds, *Biblical*, 78. Strangely, Reynolds states of the phrase *yith-addam* (Prov. 23:31): "There was no other word in the ancient languages in which the Bible was written for alcohol or for alcoholic beverages" (p. 9). How then can he turn around and present such a vigorous argument for *chemer*?

Reynolds suggests for a clear definition of non-fermented wine is lacking in all the crucial biblical passages.

9. TALMUDIC DESCRIPTION

Some prohibitionists point to the "first fruits" offering as evidence that *fermented* wine is not acceptable to God as an offering. This involves a misunderstanding of the notion of a "first fruit." It does not necessarily mean the *youngest* fruit appearing first, but may mean the first of the finished product.

Edersheim observes in this regard: "Authorities distinguish between the *Biccurim* (*primitiva*) or first fruits offered in their natural state, and the *Terumoth* (*primitae*), brought not as raw products, but in a prepared state, — as flour, oil, wine, etc."[49] We read of this practice in the Talmud at Terumoth 1:4: "Heave-offering may not be given from olives instead of from oil, or from grapes instead of from wine." In Maaseroth 1:7 we learn that "wine [is liable to the tithe] after it has been skimmed." This skimming refers to removing the scum that appears on the surface of bubbling, fermenting wine.

Thus, looking back upon the last nine points, we see from a variety of angles that *yayin* in the Bible is a fermented drink. Our nine-fold argument for identifying *yayin* as an alcoholic beverage presents a stronger case by far than the prohibitionist argument from silence. Yet having surveyed all the previous data, we must now note the remarkable and irrefutable fact that this alcoholic *yayin* is also used in Scripture in a number of righteous ways.

YAYIN AND CELEBRATION

Godly men present *yayin* as a gift in celebrating glorious events. The mysterious Old Testament figure Melchizedek was a "priest of God Most High" (Gen. 14:18). At the very least he was a type of Christ (Ps. 110:1-7; Heb. 5:6, 10; 6:20); some even argue that he may even have been a pre-incarnate, theophanic manifestation of Christ.[50] In Genesis 14:18-20 this "priest of God Most High" gave *yayin* to Abraham, the faithful "friend of God":

> And Melchizedek king of Salem brought out bread and wine; now he was a priest of God Most High. And he blessed him and said, "Blessed be Abram of God Most High, Possessor of heaven and earth; And blessed be God Most High, who has delivered your enemies into your hand." And he gave him a tenth of all.

This righteous "priest of God" offers wine in the very context of divine blessing and without the least inkling of disapprobation.

In fact, abstentionist R. Laird Harris even admits, "Of course for lack of full knowledge of the means of preservation, light fermented wine was actually a common article in Palestine and was widely used." Though he continues, "but that does not mean it was God's best for them, nor that He approved it."[51] Harris is correct in noting the *fact* of the common use of wine in Israel, though he is surely incorrect in his *interpretation* of the fact.

YAYIN AND WORSHIP

Surprising for some, God commands *yayin* as an offering in Old Testament worship. The Law of God frequently alludes to this practice:

> Now this is what you shall offer on the altar ... one-tenth of an ephah of fine flour mixed with one-fourth of a hin of beaten oil, and one-fourth of a hin of wine for a libation with one lamb. (Ex. 29:38, 40)

Its grain offering shall then be two-tenths of an ephah of fine flour mixed with oil, an offering by fire to the LORD for a soothing aroma, with its libation, a fourth of a hin of wine. (Lev. 23:13)

And you shall prepare wine for the libation, one-fourth of a hin, with the burnt offering or for the sacrifice, for each lamb ... and for the libation you shall offer one-third of a hin of wine as a soothing aroma to the LORD ... and you shall offer as the libation one-half a hin of wine as an offering by fire, as a soothing aroma to the LORD. (Num. 15:5, 7, 10)

And their libations shall be half a hin of wine for a bull and a third of a hin for the ram and a fourth of a hin for a lamb; this is the burnt offering of each month throughout the months of the year. (Num. 28:14)

In fact, the Lord instructs the Levites to take a portion of the wine offerings for their personal use (Num. 18:12, 27, 30).

This factor has a double significance for the present discussion. On the one hand, if wine were considered evil, the question arises: Why would God require wine as an offering to himself? On the other hand, if he commands it as an offering, obviously he requires his people in the Old Testament to produce it — at least for sacrificial purposes.

YAYIN AND DIVINE BLESSING

Inspired writers of Scripture consider *yayin* a gracious blessing of God. If the Israelites faithfully differentiate between clean and unclean animals (Deut. 14:3-21), tithe to the Lord (v. 22), and live obediently before him (v. 23), then God promises that they "may spend the money for whatever your heart desires, for oxen, or sheep, or wine, or strong drink, or whatever your heart desires; and there you shall eat in the presence of the LORD your God and rejoice, you and your household" (v. 26).

Psalm 104:14-15 informs us that God graciously:

> causes the grass to grow for the cattle,
> And vegetation for the labor of man,
> So that he may bring forth food from the earth,
> And wine which makes man's heart glad,
> So that he may make his face glisten with oil,
> And food which sustains man's heart.

Interestingly, here wine is joined with food and oil as a blessing; whereas, in Proverbs 23:20-21 food and wine — when overindulged in — serve as a curse. Thus again, we must distinguish between *use* and *abuse*. In fact, a moderate "gladdening of the heart" is not forbidden, according to this and other scriptures (Ps. 104:15; Eccl. 9:7; 10:19; Zech. 9:15; 10:7; Judg. 9:13).

Before considering other such references, I must note that Reynolds objects to using Psalm 104 as if *wine* is the blessing from God. He argues rather that *grape juice* is implied: "It is meaningful that in this passage the foods mentioned come from the earth.... Yeast does not come from the earth in this sense. It may be air-borne." He concludes that the passage is here speaking of "bread and wine which have not been worked on by the micro-organisms we call yeast."[52] In this same context, he notes, "Alcohol in wine is an additive, and is not a product of the earth. It comes rather from an air-borne micro-organism, and is not commended in Psalm 104:14-15."[53]

This maneuver, though ingenious, simply will not hold. In the first place, Psalm 104 is *poetic*. Poetry allows license in dealing with historical realities. It may be that yeast (which causes fermentation) is *airborne*, but the fact remains that the grapes and their juice derive "from the earth." This is the psalmist's point. In fact, "bread" does not spring forth from the earth, but obviously requires man's labor in processing the wheat, yet the psalmist speaks as if bread arises from the earth. In the second place, I really doubt whether the technical, scientific specifics of airborne yeast transport is a concern to the psalmist. The airborne yeast, in fact, grows naturally on the skin of each grape; fermentation starts the moment the skin is broken, the moment the juice comes forth. Absent pasteurization, fermentation is unavoidable. Reynolds' view is simply unnatural. Besides that, where does yeast come from in the first place? It does not arrive here from space! It, too, is ultimately land-based, an organism created by God.

Returning to passages speaking of the blessing of God in wine, we find in Ecclesiastes 9 that Solomon expounds the theme that men are in the almighty hand of God. In verse 7 he exhorts them: "Go then, eat your bread in happiness, and drink your wine with a cheerful heart; for God has already approved your works."

Isaiah 55:1 likens God's gracious offer of mercy to the free reception of water, milk — and *wine*:

> Ho! Every one who thirsts, come to the waters;
> And you who have no money come, buy and eat.
> Come, buy wine and milk
> Without money and without cost.

In one place where the oppression of the Jews ceases for a time, we read of their *improved* conditions: "Then all the Jews returned from all the places to which they had been driven away and came to the land of Judah, to Gedaliah at Mizpah, and gathered in wine and summer fruit in great abundance" (Jer. 40:12). Abundant wine is a good sign of things going well (1 Chr. 12:40; 2 Chr. 31:5; Neh. 5:18; Ezek. 27:18).

Thus, by extension *yayin* fittingly symbolizes the joyful blessings (Ps. 104:14-15) of the coming Messianic era. In Amos 9:13-15 we read:

> "Behold, days are coming," declares the LORD,
> "When the plowman will overtake the reaper
> And the treader of grapes him who sows seed;
> When the mountains will drip sweet wine,
> And all the hills will be dissolved.
> Also I will restore the captivity of my people Israel,
> And they will rebuild the ruined cities and live in them,
> They will also plant vineyards and drink their wine,
> And make gardens and eat their fruit.
> I will also plant them on their land,
> And they will not again be rooted out from their land
> Which I have given them,"
> Says the LORD your God.

Isaiah puts the matter this way:

> And the LORD of hosts will prepare a lavish banquet for all peoples on this mountain;
> A banquet of aged wine, choice pieces with marrow,
> And refined, aged wine.
> And on this mountain He will swallow up the covering which is over all peoples,
> Even the veil which is stretched over all nations.
> He will swallow up death for all time,
> And the Lord GOD will wipe tears away from all faces,
> And He will remove the reproach of His people from all the earth;
> For the LORD has spoken.
> And it will be said in that day, "Behold, this is our God for whom we have waited that He might save us.
> This is the LORD for whom we have waited;
> Let us rejoice and be glad in His salvation." (25:6-9)

YAYIN AND DIVINE CURSE

In anger and expressing his divine curse the Lord removes *yayin* from Israel. Deuteronomy 28 is a most significant chapter dealing with God's covenant with Israel. The first fourteen verses outline concrete covenantal blessings God grants to Israel if they are obedient. Verses 15 through 68 outline concrete aspects of God's curse consequent upon Israel's disobedience to God. For the present study, verse 39 is most instructive: "You shall plant and cultivate vineyards, but you shall neither drink of the wine nor gather the grapes, for the worm shall devour them." God's curse would remove *all* good things from the disobedient culture: farm animals (v. 31), covenant children (vv. 32, 41), agricultural produce (vv. 33, 38, 42), olive trees (v. 40), grape vines and wine (v. 39).

Having surveyed various commendations of *yayin*, I should note before moving on to other matters that Scripture often employs *yayin* metaphorically in a bad sense. Just as leaven can symbolize evil's penetrating, corrupting power (Matt. 16:6; 1 Cor. 5:8), so wine can serve as a metaphor of something disastrous: the wrath of God against his enemies (Ps. 60:5, 7; 78:65; Jer. 25:15). Yet, just as leaven may represent good influences (Lev. 7:13; 23:17; Matt. 13:33), *yayin* can just as easily symbolize something good: godly wisdom (Prov. 9:2-5), the joy of human love (Song 5:1), and the gospel of God's saving grace (Is. 55:1).

Reynolds argues for prohibition on the basis of such "negative" passages. For instance, Micah 2:11 reads:

> If a man walking after wind and falsehood
> Had told lies and said, "I will speak out to you concerning wine and liquor,"
> He would be spokesman to this people.

He suggests that "the inference is inescapable that God holds in contempt preachers who preach in favor of alcoholic beverages even in normal times."[54] Reynolds' observation is woefully inaccurate. The negative function here is due to the prophet's promising good things (wine) *rather than* warning of God's coming judgment. It parallels in sense Isaiah 30:10-11 where Israel seeks prophets who speak "pleasant words" *rather than* truth.

THE HEBREW TERM *TIROSH*

The Hebrew word *tirosh* is the Old Testament's second most frequently occurring word for "wine," appearing thirty-eight times. It properly designates the "must, fresh, or new wine."[55] The *King James Version* most often translates it as either "wine" or "new wine." Van Impe states that it "means new wine or grape juice."[56]

Technically, *tirosh* is a form of immature *yayin*, an early stage in the fermentation process. When linked with "corn" (*daghn*) in the Old Testament, it often emphasizes these elements — grain and grapes — as the raw products out of which the finished products of bread and wine arise.[57] This clearly appears in Genesis 27:28:

> Now may God give you of the dew of heaven,
> And of the fatness of the earth,
> And an abundance of grain and new wine.

On the other hand, "bread" (*lechem*) is found in conjunction with "wine" (*yayin*), as in many other Old Testament passages (Gen.14:18; Deut. 29:6; Judg.19:19; 1 Sam.10:3; 16:20; 25:18; 2 Sam.16:1-2; Neh. 5:15; Prov. 4:17; Eccl. 9:7; Hos. 9:4; Hag. 2:12). *Lechem* and *yayin* are the finished products made from *daghn* and *tirosh*. This does not, however, preclude *tirosh* from possessing intoxicating qualities. According to the *International Standard Bible Encyclopedia*:

> Unfermented grape juice is a very difficult thing to keep without the aid of modern antiseptic precautions, and its preservation in the warm and not over cleanly conditions of ancient Palestine was impossible. Consequently *tirosh* came to mean wine that was not fully aged (although with full intoxicating properties, Judg. 9:13; Hos. 4:11; Acts 2:13) or wine when considered specifically as the product of grapes (Deut. 12:17; 18:4).[58]

In fact, *tirosh* derives from the Hebrew stem *yarash*, which means "take possession of, inherit, dispossess." Thus, as the Brown-Driver-Briggs lexicon notes, *tirosh* can be either "enlivening" or "injurious."[59] Reynolds even admits:

> As to the idea that *tirosh* is so called because it possesses the mind, that it takes over and perverts the normal mental functions, this ought not to be dismissed as utterly unreasonable. Gesenius-Buhl says under the word *yarash* (to take possession) that *tirosh* may be a derivative. Koehler-Baumgardner says it is without doubt a derivative. If it is, the case for assuming that *tirosh* was primally an intoxicant is greatly strengthened.[60]

He continues, "If so, the idea of the ancient people who gave the beverage that name may have been to call it 'that which takes possession.'"[61]

Hosea 4 speaks of the moral degradation of Israel in multiplying her sins before God (v. 7). Then in verse 11 the prophet laments that "harlotry, wine, and new wine [*tirosh*] take away the understanding." That is, men are intoxicated by "new wine," as well as by "wine" (*yayin*). The *New Bible Dictionary* comments, "Ho. 4:11, together with the usage of the Talmud, makes clear that it is capable of being used in a bad sense."[62]

But, just as with *yayin*, *tirosh* can be used righteously. In Genesis 27:28 and 37 Isaac blesses Jacob by calling on God to bless him with "abundance of grain and new wine" (*tirosh*). It often appears as an explicit blessing of God, as in the following Scripture passages:

> And He will love you and bless you and multiply you; He will also bless the fruit of your womb and the fruit of your ground, your grain and your new wine. (Deut. 7:13)

> He will give the rain for your land in its season, the early and late rain, that you may gather in your grain and your new wine and your oil. (Deut. 11:14)

> So your barns will be filled with plenty, and your vats will overflow with new wine. (Prov. 3:10)

> The LORD has sworn by His right hand and by His strong arm, "I will never again give your grain as food for your enemies; nor will foreigners drink your new wine, for which you have labored." (Is. 62:8)

> For what comeliness and beauty will be theirs! Grain will make the young men flourish, and new wine the virgins. (Zech. 9:17)

Removal of new wine (*tirosh*) from the land is an aspect of God's curse which "shall eat the offspring of your herd and the produce of your ground until you are destroyed, who also leaves you no grain, new wine, or oil, nor the increase of your herd or the young of your flock until they have caused you to perish" (Deut. 28:51; Is. 24:7; Hos. 2:9; 9:2; Joel 1:10; Hag. 1:11).

THE HEBREW TERM *SHEKAR*

This word occurs twenty-two times in the Old Testament and literally means "intoxicating drink, strong drink."[63] It is based on the verb *shakar*, which means "to be, or become, drunk, drunken."[64] According to the *Theological Wordbook of the Old Testament* the verb means "to intoxicate" in numerous passages.[65] It is related to the word *shikkar* ("drunkard"[66]) and *shikkaron* ("drunkenness"[67]). The *International Standard Bible Encyclopedia* notes that *shekar* "appears to mean 'intoxicating drink' of any sort."[68]

As the *Theological Workbook of the Old Testament* points out, "With very few exceptions *shakar* and its derivatives are used in a highly unfavorable and negative context. But a few passages where the root is used in an acceptable sense should be observed: Numbers 28:7; Deuteronomy 14:26; and Proverbs 31:6."[69] Abstentionist Harris agrees: "*shekar* meaning intoxicating drinks, a word which is almost universally used with an evil connotation."[70]

Furthermore, we should note:

> With the exception of Numbers 28:7, "strong drink" is always coupled with "wine." The two terms are commonly used as mutually exclusive, and as together exhaustive of all kinds of intoxicants.... Thus, *shekar* is a comprehensive term for all kinds of fermented drinks [i.e., from dates, apples, barley, etc.], excluding wine.[71]

Not only may we demonstrate etymologically that *shekar* possesses the potential to inebriate, but most versions translate the word to indicate as much: "strong drink" *(New American Standard Bible, King James Version, American Standard Version)*, "intoxicating drink" (*New King James Version*), "liquor" *(Moffatt)*, "hard liquor" *(Living Bible)*, "beer" *(New International Version)*, and so forth.

Even beyond basic etymological considerations and translational consensus, however, the Scripture itself records instances of either actual or alleged cases of drunkenness resulting from imbibing *shekar*. In 1 Samuel 1:12-15 Eli accuses Hannah of being drunk because of her unusual conduct:

> Now it came about, as she continued praying before the LORD, that Eli was watching her mouth. As for Hannah, she was speaking in her heart, only her lips were moving, but her voice was not heard. So Eli thought she was drunk. Then Eli said to her, "How long will you make yourself drunk? Put away your wine from you." But Hannah answered and said, "No, my lord, I am a woman oppressed in spirit; I have drunk neither wine nor strong drink [*shekar*], but I have poured out my soul before the LORD."

In the well-known Proverbs 20:1 passage, *shekar* is a "brawler" in that it has the potential to spur a troublesome, contentious spirit in the drunkard. In Isaiah 5:11 a woe is called down upon those who seek to be drunken with an immoderate use either of wine or of strong drink:

> Woe to those who rise early in the morning that they may pursue strong drink;
> Who stay up late in the evening that wine may inflame them!

Kerr comments that in light of such passages, "the attempt made to prove that it was simply the unfermented juice of certain fruits is quite without foundation."[72]

Yet, God never universally prohibits or discourages it. Rather he commands *shekar* as a drink-offering. Numbers 28:7 reads, "Then the libation with it shall be a fourth of a hin for each lamb, in the holy place you shall pour out a libation of strong drink [*shekar*] to the LORD." This is significant in that it implies both its manufacture and production by devout Jews, and in that it can be an offering to the Lord.

Finally we come to the *locus classicus* in the debate over

shekar and its toleration in God's law — Deuteronomy 14:22-26, where Moses defines the "rejoicing tithe":

> You shall surely tithe all the produce from what you sow, which comes out of the field every year. And you shall eat in the presence of the LORD your God, at the place where He chooses to establish His name, the tithe of your grain, your new wine, your oil, and the first-born of your herd and your flock, in order that you may learn to fear the LORD your God always. And if the distance is so great for you that you are not able to bring the tithe ... then you shall exchange it for money.... And you may spend the money for whatever your heart desires, for oxen, or sheep, or wine, or strong drink [*shekar*], or whatever your heart desires; and there you shall eat in the presence of the LORD your God and rejoice, you and your household.

The thrust of this passage is unambiguous; the divine sanction unmistakable: Moses not only allows *shekar* among God's people, but encourages its enjoyment "in the presence of the LORD" (v. 26), if partaken in "the fear of God" (v. 23).†

† The best the prohibitionist can do with this passage is to divert attention away from it by appeal to the "analogy of Scripture" as it is understood in terms of their presuppositions. Reynolds does this on page 23 of *Alcohol and the Bible*: "Where it [*shekar*] is used in Deuteronomy 14:26 it can be argued from the general consistency of all the Scripture that it was not an intoxicant." And this despite the clear, compelling and overwhelming exegetical, translational, and contextual considerations! Reynolds' maneuver, of course, *assumes* the point in question and ignores contrary evidence.

THE HEBREW TERM *'ASIS*

This word occurs only five times in Scripture and is translated either "sweet wine," "new wine," or "juice" in *King James*; the *New American Standard* translates it "sweet wine," and the *New International* "new wine." The word itself actually means "pressed out."[73] In Malachi 4:3 (Mal. 3:21 in the Hebrew text) its verb stem speaks of God's "treading down" the wicked.

Thus, '*asis* is properly the newly expressed juice of the grape. Yet again, despite the seeming innocence of this word lexically, '*asis* can and does have the power to intoxicate. In Joel 1:5 the word of the Lord to Israel prophesies:

> Awake, drunkards, and weep;
> And wail, all you wine drinkers,
> On account of the sweet wine ['*asis*]
> That is cut off from your mouth.

In Isaiah 49:26 the metaphorical use of '*asis* demands its inebriating potential:

> And I will feed your oppressors with their own flesh,
> And they will become drunk with their own blood as with sweet wine;
> And all flesh will know that I, the LORD, am your Savior,
> And your Redeemer, the Mighty One of Jacob.

Scripture, however, employs '*asis* in two Messianic passages as emblems of God's gracious blessings. In Joel 3:18 we read, "And it will come about in that day that the mountains will drip with sweet wine and the hills will flow with milk." Interestingly, Joel uses '*asis* in both a good and a bad sense, as a comparison of this passage with the previously quoted one in the first chapter of Joel demonstrates. Likewise, Amos 9:13 promises:

> "Behold, days are coming," declares the LORD,
> "When the plowman will overtake the reaper
> And the treader of grapes him who sows seed;
> When the mountains will drip sweet wine,
> And all the hills will be dissolved."

CONCLUSION

In light of the wealth of evidence above, one must incredulously wonder at the following statement by Christian scholar and scientist Henry M. Morris: "In the Old Testament two Hebrew words ('*tirosh*' and '*yayin*') are both translated 'wine,' the former meaning the fresh juice of the grape and the latter the fermented or decayed juice.... It is significant that nowhere does the Bible actually endorse the drinking of wine or other intoxicating drink."[74] Such a statement by a prohibitionist is wholly without merit, standing against an overwhelming mass of irrefutable evidence.

The Old Testament considers *all sorts* of wines as blessings — even though they have the potential for abuse and could become a curse upon sinful man. The Old Testament knows nothing of "safe" and "unsafe" wines. It is totally silent on any supposed attempt to keep wine from undergoing natural fermentation. Nehemiah appears in Nehemiah 5 as a righteous servant of God, faithfully doing the Lord's work; in verses 16 through 19 we read Nehemiah's humble and godly plea for God's remembrance of all his conduct, a part of which was the furnishing of "all sorts of wine in abundance":

> And I also applied myself to the work on this wall; we did not buy any land, and all my servants were gathered there for the work. Moreover, there were at my table one hundred and fifty Jews and officials, besides those who came to us from the nations that were around us. Now that which was prepared for each day was one ox and six choice sheep, also birds were prepared for me; and once in ten days *all sorts of wines were furnished in abundance*. Yet for all this I did not demand the governor's food allowance, because the servitude was heavy on this people. Remember me, O my God, for good, according to all that I have done for this people [emphasis added].

The case for the moderationist position is so strong in the Old Testament that even the 1977 abstentionist report by the "Study Committee on Beverage Use of Alcohol" of the Reformed Presbyterian Church, Evangelical Synod, must admit: "The selectively specific cases of abstinence are an indicator that the Mosaic code did not make total abstinence a universally absolute rule in Israel."[75]

Abstentionist Harold Lindsell agrees when he writes, "Since the body of the believer is the temple of the Holy Spirit, it is not difficult to conclude that abstinence is to be preferred even though *there is no express prohibition in Scripture against the use of alcohol in moderation*."†

† Lindsell, 116. Emphasis mine. In effect he has declared that Scripture is not adequate today to equip us for every good work, contrary to 2 Timothy 3:16-17. This is a "holier than thou" position with a vengeance; it is "holier" than Scripture itself!

CHAPTER 4
THE NEW TESTAMENT
AND ALCOHOL USE

The New Testament is only about one-fourth the size of the Old Testament. Its historical scope — covering the period from the birth of Christ in 4 B.C. until the completion of the last New Testament book — spans only 75 to 100 years. In contrast the Old Testament material spans history from the creation until around 400 B.C. (excluding prophetic statements regarding the future), although the Old Testament canon itself dates from 1450 B.C. to 400 B.C.

Furthermore, the Old Testament is clearly foundational for, and preparational to, the New Testament in every sense of the word. In light of these factors of size, dates, and function, it should not be surprising that the material of the Old Testament relating to our study is much more abundant than that of the New Testament. This does not hurt our argument, however: In light of the fundamental unity of the two Testaments (Matt. 5:17-19; 1 Cor. 10:11), the Old Testament is as binding and ethically relevant (Rom. 3:31; 2 Tim. 3:16-17) as that of the New Testament, unless the New Testament specifically repeals a principle or practice of the Old — as in the case of the sacrificial system (Hebrews) and circumcision (Acts 15; Gal. 3-5).

Consequently, our study of the New Testament will be somewhat shorter than the foregoing. Nevertheless, I will show that the New Testament in no way contravenes the Old regarding the matter of alcohol and is, in fact, perfectly harmonious with it. Let us begin by considering two important Greek terms relevant to our study: *oinos* and *gleukos*.

THE GREEK TERM *OINOS*

Oinos occurs thirty-three times in the New Testament and all translations consistently render it "wine." It also appears in various compounds such as *oinophlugia* ("excess wine"), *paroinos* ("addicted to wine"), and *oinopotis* ("drunkard"). As in the Old Testament word studies, so is it in the New: we discover from a variety of angles a lexical consensus on the fermented quality of *oinos*.

First, *oinos* is the Greek equivalent to the Hebrew *yayin*, which we understand is fermented wine (see Chapter 3). Biblical lexicographers, for instance, J. H. Thayer[1] and G. Abbott-Smith,[2] point to its frequent use in the Septuagint as a translation for *yayin*.

Second, classical Greek — the historical forerunner of New Testament Greek — employs the term as a fermented beverage. The Liddell and Scott *Greek-English Lexicon* defines *oinos* as "the fermented juice of the grape."[3] Interestingly, classical Greek apparently uses *oinos* as a functional equivalent for "fermented juice" of all sorts. As Liddell and Scott point out, *oinos* can be used to refer to barley wine (a kind of beer), palm wine, and lotus wine — all of which are distinguished from grape-wine (*oinos ampelinos*).[4]

Third, Greek New Testament lexicographers maintain its fermented quality. The standard lexicon of our day, Arndt-Gingrich, notes that the word is "normally the fermented juice of the grape ... the word for 'must, or unfermented grape juice,' is *trux*."[5] The reputable *Illustrated Davis Bible Dictionary* agrees: "The Greek *oinos* ... means the fermented juice of the grape, except when it is qualified by the word 'new.'"[6] No major New Testament lexicon disputes the fermented character of *oinos*.

Not only does clear lexical evidence exist as to the alcoholic nature of *oinos*, but New Testament contextual evidence reinforces the matter, as well. For instance, in Ephesians 5:18 Paul exhorts the Ephesian Christians (and all Christians) to "be not drunk with wine, wherein is excess" (*King James Version*). In Paul's prerequisites for church leadership he commands that "Deacons likewise must be men of dignity, not double-tongued, or addicted to much wine" (1 Tim. 3:8), and that "older women likewise are to be reverent in their behavior, not malicious gossips, not enslaved to much wine" (Titus 2:3). These statements imply the alcoholic nature of *oinos* beyond a shadow of doubt.

The case is clear: *oinos* is an alcoholic beverage. Yet, nowhere does the New Testament forbid it. As already hinted at above, Scripture does not require ordained church officers to abstain from it. The specific requirement regarding wine use among office holders and candidates for office is that which characterizes the moderationist position.

In 1 Timothy 3:3 and Titus 1:7 the requirement for the office of elder is that the candidate be "not addicted to wine." In 1 Timothy 3:8 the moral obligation for the office of deacon is that the candidate not be "addicted to much wine." In the former case, the word used is *paroinos*, which Thayer notes refers to "one who sits long at his wine, given to wine, drunken."[7] In the latter case the injunction reads: *me oino pollo prosechontas* (literally: "not wine much devoted to," i.e., "not devoted to much wine").[8]

In the aforementioned texts the references to "much" (*pollo*) and "devoted" (*prosechontas*) are both important. "Much" deals with the amount of intake; "devoted" speaks of the inordinate, immoderate attachment to wine. Most significantly we note that Paul refrains from a total prohibition for officers of the church. He only forbids abuse of alcoholic beverages. (Who could say he was commanding officers not to be "devoted to much" grape juice?) No apostle ever commands anything along the lines of: "Drink no wine at all." The commands are clearly along the lines of: "Be not drunk with wine" (Eph. 5:18); "be not addicted to much wine" (1 Tim. 3:8); "be not enslaved to wine" (Titus 2:3); and so on.

Some prohibitionists offer an interesting but ultimately futile attempt to argue that Paul speaks of wine as something evil itself. Reynolds is a case in point:

> "Be not drunk with wine in which is debauchery." Some commentators say that the words "in which" refer to the whole phrase, "Be not drunk with wine," and not just to "wine." The wish not to accept the idea that debauchery is "in" wine makes them reject this obvious sense, and choose instead the idea that it lies in being drunk.[9]

Let us note in the first place the obvious problem with such a statement: As mentioned above, why did not Paul simply command: "Drink no wine, wherein is excess"? Why does the apostle consistently add such limiting notions to the act of drinking, such as "be not drunk," "not addicted to," and "not enslaved to"? Further, I would point out that no commentators or lexicographers suggest Reynolds' interpretation. For instance, *The Expositor's Greek New Testament* observes, "The *en ho* refers not to the *oinos* alone (which might infer a Gnostic view of matter or Montanistic, ascetic ideas of life), but to the whole phrase *methuskesthe oino* — the becoming drunk with wine."[10]

It further adds:

The contrast, as most commentators recognise, is not merely between the *oino* and the *pneumatic* but between the *methuskesthe* and the *plerousthe*. Otherwise the order would have been *me oino methuskesthe, all en pneumati plerousthe* (Meyer). The contrast is not between the instruments but between the states — between two elevated states, one due to the excitement of wine, the other to the inspiration and enlightenment of the Spirit.[11]

Thus, in this more common interpretation the situation contrasts thus:

Be not drunk with wine, in which is excess,
Be filled with the Spirit, speaking to yourselves in psalms

Consequently, *when drunk* with wine, one is in excess (riot, etc.). But when *filled with the Spirit*, he engages in speaking psalms. It seems that the Greek *asotia* ("excess") relates better to the verbal idea in that it derives from the privative *a* + *sozo*, which together literally mean "not saved." The New Testament reckons the *drunkard* "unsavable," as it were, not those who merely *drink*. For such *drunkards* "shall not inherit the kingdom of God" (1 Cor. 6:9; Gal. 5:21).

It would not at all adversely affect the moderationist position, however, to allow Reynolds' interpretation. I agree that the Scripture poetically calls wine a "mocker/brawler" (Prov. 20:1). And I do not deny that wine can cause "excess/ riot" (see Chapter 2). The potential and the power certainly reside therein. I would simply point out that Paul commands Christians not to be *drunk* with it; he does not urge us to "drink (*pino*) no wine, wherein is excess." Nowhere is such a command ever given. The command is "be not drunk." I agree with the leading commentators that the phrase "in which is excess" naturally relates to the negative prohibition: "Be not drunk."

THE GREEK TERM *GLEUKOS*

This word occurs only once in the New Testament, in Acts 2:13. According to Thayer, it means, "must, the sweet juice pressed from the grape ... sweet wine."[12] As Thayer notes, "It is strange that this word, which probably" refers only to unfermented beverage occurs only once. The insertion of the tentative "probably" is necessary because in its only occurrence in the New Testament it is used in a *mocking allegation* that the disciples were drunk on it: Acts 2:13. Many lexicographers allow that it could well include fermented wine in its connotation. But assuming for a moment that it is unfermented juice — as opposed to *oinos*, which obviously refers to an alcoholic beverage — why does not the Lord commend *gleukos* as a moral alternative to the consumption of *oinos*? This question is not, of course, significant to our study; sometimes to ask a question is to answer it.

JESUS DRANK WINE

The Lord Jesus Christ lived in a culture that used wine as a common, everyday beverage.[13] Although our Lord spoke out against drunkenness as a sinful condition (Matt. 24:29; Luke 12:45; 21:34), he never disparaged the drinking of wine (*oinos*) per se. If he had, he would then not only be at variance with the Old Testament, which he affirms as the unfailing Word of God, but he would also have been guilty of hypocrisy.

In Luke 7:33-35 Jesus refers to his practice of drinking wine as a vivid illustration of a distinctive difference between himself and his forerunner, John the Baptist:

> For John the Baptist has come eating no bread and drinking no wine; and you say, "He has a demon!" The Son of Man

has come eating and drinking; and you say, "Behold, a gluttonous man, and a drunkard, a friend of tax-gatherers and sinners." Yet wisdom is vindicated by all her children.

Some Christians maintain that this citation does not state that Jesus did, in fact, drink wine. They place particular emphasis on the fact that although he specifically mentioned "wine" (*oinos*) when referring to John, he does *not* use the word "wine" when speaking of himself. This attempt to avoid the obvious, however, is unsuccessful for two reasons:

First, commentators widely agree that the intent is to parallel the two statements. Consequently, this demands that we assume "wine" in the second, abbreviated part of the parallelism. The accusations Jesus presented are set in antithetic parallelism, where a thought is expressed by contrasting it with its opposite. Here the contrast is between *not* "eating and drinking" and "eating and drinking."

Reynolds admits the parallelism but maintains that the contrast was over John's "Naziritic" abstinence from "non-alcoholic products of the grape"[14] and Jesus' partaking of such. This assertion is tenuous, at best. In the first place, that John was a Nazirite is only a conjecture based on slight intimation. No biblical statement declares him a Nazirite. In the allegedly similar case of Samson we read specifically that he was to "be a Nazirite to God from the womb" (Judg. 13:7). The Gospel record conspicuously lacks such a declaration.

Neither do we discover John keeping *any other* of the various Naziritic strictures revealed in Numbers 6. For instance, God does not instruct John's parents to avoid cutting his hair (Num. 6:5, Judg. 13:5). Nor do we find a record of the Baptist's having long hair in the several descriptions of him (Matt. 3:4; 11:8; Mark 1:6).

Furthermore, the angel instructs John's father in Luke

1:15 only to restrict him from partaking of "wine" (*oinos*) and "strong drink" (*sikera*). In light of the immediate context, the practice seems designed to encourage a special infilling of the Holy Spirit (compare v. 15 with Eph. 5:18). John is not denied "must" (*trux*) or "sweet new wine" (*gleukos*). And it is the wine matter that Christ particularly mentions in Luke 7.

Second, if Jesus did not drink wine, how could his assailants allege he is a drunkard? Why did he not point out that they were mistaken in their assertion that he drank? If you did not drink wine, yet someone accused you of being a drunkard, what would your most obvious response be?

JESUS MADE WINE

While attending the marriage feast in Cana of Galilee, Jesus miraculously "manufactured" a high-quality wine (John 2:1-11). The quantity was upwards of six firkins (about 120 gallons) for the wedding party and guests.

Some object to using this miracle in supporting the moderationist argument. They argue that both the wine that ran out and the miraculously produced wine are actually grape juice. Harris, for instance, notes that the sheer volume of the Christ-produced wine (120 gallons) demands its non-fermented quality: Otherwise Jesus would be creating too much alcoholic wine for such a small party — and thereby encouraging drunkenness.†

† Harris, 12. But why must we assume the party was "small"? After all, Jesus *does* create upwards of 120 gallons of some kind of beverage. Was this sheer extravagance and waste?

But this defies the facts, for the word *oinos* describes both wines in question. We have already seen that this word indicates a fermented quality drink, i.e., wine. Furthermore, William Hendriksen comments that due to the season of the wedding — just before Spring Passover (John 2:13) — the wine would naturally be fermented. The grape harvest would have been collected over six months earlier, in September. Thus, the wine had ample time to ferment.[15]

In his characteristically innovative style, Reynolds interprets the occasion along wholly different lines:

> The situation appears to have been as follows: The wedding party had been indulging in cheap, foul tasting wine, made perhaps partly from diseased grapes, and having a high alcoholic content. The people were drunk and behaving in a manner which moved to righteous indignation our Lord who was and is absolutely and totally pure of mind and body. His mother's sorrow that the party had run out of that sort of wine and her implied suggestion that He provide more of the same caused Him in righteous sorrow to speak stern words to her which have much puzzled Bible commentators.[16]

Elsewhere he surmises that "it may be that Christ miraculously healed their bodies of a craving for alcohol."[17]

Stripped of the imaginative conjecture (wine from diseased grapes and the unwarranted assumption that Jesus heals them from their *taste* for alcohol), Reynolds basically establishes his case upon the following considerations: (1) Jesus severely rebuked his mother (v. 4), indicating his displeasure at her bringing him to such a riotous feast; (2) based on verse 10 in the Greek, "the people at the wedding party were already intoxicated"; (3) the governor of the feast who "had surely not become drunk" recognized the new drink as the "best wine (grape juice).... This he said as a connoisseur of choice vintage without regard to alcoholic content"; and (4) with so much drunkenness involved, it would be morally intolerable for Christ to provide such a large quantity of alcoholic wine.[18]

In considering the merits of Reynolds' argument, we should note in the first place that his interpretation of Jesus' rebuke of Mary is questionable. Commentators throughout

Christian history have inconclusively debated the rationale of his rebuke. Not only so, but Reynolds' (questionable) interpretation implicates Mary in a surprising tolerance of evil conduct. This is quite out of character for her according to the biblical record elsewhere.

Reynolds' suggestion is even more out of character for Jesus. Why did he not rebuke those who are drunk, since he regularly confronted sin in the sinner (John 4:17-19; 8:11)? Or the governor of such a feast, since Jesus warned of responsibility inhering in positions of authority (Matt. 23:12; Luke 12:48)? Why did Jesus do anything *at all* to assist them in their partying, since he overturned the tables of those acting sinfully in the Temple (Matt. 21:12-13)? Why did he stay around until the wine ran out?†

Still further, if Jesus is rebuking Mary, why does she immediately (v. 5) urge the servants to prepare for some miracle or otherwise positive action from Jesus? You would think a rebuke to a request would *discourage* one from hoping for a positive result.

† Reynolds' answers this question by asserting that Mary and Jesus "probably arrive late" (*Biblical*, 97). Of course, this is only conjecture and totally without biblical warrant.

A more plausible interpretation of Jesus' response relates to the fact that he was just beginning his Messianic ministry (John 2:11). Consequently, it was then time for Mary to cease looking upon him as her son and to begin recognizing him as her Lord and Savior (Mark 3:33-34).[19]

Next, Reynolds seems both to misinterpret and to misapply the governor's statement and to overstate his own lexical case. The governor did not say that those at this particular party were "drunk." Rather, he was stating a general practice among those who host feasts: "Every man serves the good wine first, and when men have drunk freely, then that which is poorer." Many commentators understand this along the lines proposed by J. C. Ellicott: "There is clearly no reference to the present feast. It is a coarse jest of the ruler's, the sort of remark that forms part of the stock in trade of a hired manager of banquets."[20]

In addition, the Greek text does not demand the translation Reynolds urges (although it is lexically possible). Reynolds says in regard to the term *methusthosin* in verse 10, "There is little to support the idea that this is not said in reference to the wedding party, or that it does not mean that they were intoxicated."[21]

He continues:

> From the expressions used in modern English translations it might be understood that the wedding party had drunk enough to remove some of their thirst, but were still sober and were behaving decorously. The Greek word *methuo* does not allow such an interpretation. Liddell and Scott's highly respected Greek English Lexicon says it means "to be drunken".... In no passage in the Bible or out of it does it mean to have quenched the thirst while remaining sober.[22]

Not only does Reynolds by his own admission set himself against the consensus of "modern English translations" (no Bible translation renders the verb as indicating drunkenness), but he apparently has not carefully researched the matter. Certainly the *methuo* word group generally indicates drunkenness; this is its preponderate and primary usage. But that is not its only meaning or function, contrary to Reynolds' sweeping assertion.

The standard Arndt-Gingrich lexicon notes under the *methuo* entry that it can mean "drink freely" and lists John 2:10 as a demonstration of that usage. Linguist Herbert Preisker in the authoritative *Theological Dictionary of the New Testament* makes the following observations on this word group and on John 2:10 in particular: *"methusko* can often be used for a refreshing drink [as in Greek literature] 'I will refresh the souls of the priests.'"[23] And he adds further, "Philo commends *methe* and *methuein* for the wise man as the drinking of wine, not to excess (*aden*) nor unmixed (*akraton*) ... but with moderation and joy."[24] Then Preisker approaches the passage in question: "*Methuo* and *methuskomai* are mostly used lit[erally] in the NT for 'to be drunk' and 'to get drunk.' *Methuskomai* is used with no ethical or religious judgment in Jn. 2:10 in connection with the rule that the poorer wine is served only when the guests have drunk well."[25]

Other technical lexical tools cite the Septuagint usage of the *methuo* word group in various Old Testament passages as illustrating this fact. For instance, the Parkhurst lexicon is very clear:

> *Methuo.* It denotes in general to drink wine or strong drink more freely than usual, and that whether to drunkenness or not.... Passively: To drink freely and to cheerfulness, though not to drunkenness... John 2:10. And in this sense the verb is plainly used by the LXX [i.e. Septuagint], Gen. 43:34; Cant. 5:1.[26]

Finally, Reynolds' statement regarding the governor's acting as a "connoisseur of choice vintage without regard to alcoholic content" is purely gratuitous, being based on Reynolds' preconceived ideas imported into the text.

In the first place, it goes against the well-nigh universal prevalence of man's preferring old (fermented) wine over new wine (unfermented grape juice?). The Lord refers to this assessment among men in Luke 5:39: "And no one, after drinking old wine wishes for new; for he says, 'The old is good enough.'" Of this statement Reynolds argues that "only the natural man with corrupted taste" prefers fermented wine.[27]

Heinrich Seeseman notes that preference for old wine was prevalent among Jewish writers (see Sir. 9:10; Ber. 51), as well as Greek and Roman authors (cf. Lucianus, *De Mercede Conductis*; Plutarchus, *De Mario*; Plautus, *Casina*).[28] For instance, Columello wrote in the first century, "Almost every wine has the property of acquiring excellence with age."[29] This assessment remains true throughout history. Francis Bacon wrote in 1623, "Alonso of Aragon was wont to say in commendation of age, that age appears to be best in four things — old wood best to burn, old wine to drink, old friends to trust, and old authors to read" (*Apothogems*, No. 206). Similarly, playwright John Webster penned in 1607, "Is not old wine wholesomest?" (*Westward Hoe*, Act II, Sc. ii.)

In the second place, assuming these folks were drunk (Reynolds' analysis), why did they not prefer alcoholic wine? Why would the (allegedly) drunken headmaster declare Jesus' wine "better," since he was in the "party spirit"? After all, Reynolds argues that "the natural man with corrupted taste" prefers fermented wine. You would think that drunken men at a riotous party would exhibit the "natural man's" preference for fermented beverage when analyzing Jesus' wine.

Even Messianic prophecies use the imagery of "aged" (old, fermented) wine at banquets as illustrating that which is good. Isaiah 25:6 says, "And the LORD of hosts will prepare a lavish banquet for all peoples on this mountain; a banquet of aged wine, choice pieces with marrow, and refined, aged wine."

I believe these bases should inform us of the meaning of the governor's statement: "You have kept the good wine until now." Both the original wine and the miraculously produced wine are called *oinos*, which means "fermented grape juice," or alcoholic wine.

COMMUNION AND WINE

The Lord Jesus Christ institutes the Last Supper with wine — not grape juice. We may easily demonstrate this in the light of both exegetical and cultural considerations.

Oftentimes we hear prohibitionists suggesting that fermented wine would be precluded from the Passover because it contains yeast/leaven. But this is mistaken. Even as Reynolds admits, "A modern Jewish Rabbi had advised me that modern Jews make a distinction between ferment, which is permitted at Passover, and leaven, which is not."[30]

Prohibitionists also point out that Jesus consistently speaks of "the cup" being filled with "the fruit of the vine" — not *oinos* (Matt. 26:29; Mark 14:25; Luke 22:18). But "the fruit of the vine" is the functional equivalent of "wine." If taken literally, the phrase would lead to an absurdity: it would teach that the cup is filled with uncrushed whole grapes! The observations from the following authorities, however, should help clear up this mistaken notion.

Dunlop Moore writes:

> The expression the "fruit of the vine" is employed by our Saviour in the synoptical Gospels to denote the element contained in the cup of the Holy Supper. The fruit of the vine is literally the grape. But the Jews from time immemorial have used this phrase to designate the wine partaken of on sacred occasions, as at the Passover and on the evening of the Sabbath. The Mishna (*De. Bened*, cap. 6, pars I) expressly states, that, in pronouncing blessings, "the fruit of the vine" is the consecrated expression for *yayin*.... The Christian Fathers, as well as the Jewish rabbis, have understood "the fruit of the vine" to mean wine in the proper sense. Our Lord, in instituting the Supper after the Passover, availed himself of the expression invariably employed by his countrymen in speaking of the wine of the Passover. On other occasions, when employing the language of common life, he calls wine by its ordinary name.[31]

Davis' *Dictionary* agrees:

> Fruit of the vine, the designation used by Jesus at the institution of the Lord's Supper ... is the expression employed by the Jews from time immemorial for the wine partaken of on sacred occasions, as at the Passover and on the evening of the Sabbath (Mishna, *Berakoth*, vi. 1). The Greeks also used the term as a synonym of wine which was capable of producing intoxication (Herod I. 211, 212).[32]

Heinrich Seeseman notes of the phrase "fruit of the vine" (*genema tes ampelou*), "It is obvious ... that according to custom Jesus was proffering wine in the cup over which He pronounced the blessing; this may be seen especially from the solemn *genema tes ampelou* ... which was borrowed from Judaism."[33]

For additional information along these lines, consult the following scholars: Friedrich Buschel, Johannes Behm, and G. Dalman.[34] Indeed, in pagan antiquity "the fruit of the vine" can and does mean alcoholic wine, as we discover in Herodotus (*Histories* 1:211, 212). This may be helpful in explaining the problem of drunkenness at communion services in the troublesome Corinthian church (1 Cor. 11:21-22).

CONCLUSION

As I did when concluding the survey of the Old Testament, I close this study of the New Testament evidence with a telling admission by an abstentionist publication: "From the example and teaching of Jesus and the teaching of Paul, it cannot be certainly concluded that total abstinence was a requirement in the New Testament church."[35] And if it were not a requirement in the apostolic church, why should it *now* be a requirement? Scripture is our final authority in the realm of ethics and morality.

CHAPTER 5
ALLEGED
NEGATIVE PASSAGES

Before moving on into the matter of Christian liberty, which is more directly related to the abstentionist position, I believe it will be helpful to consider the passages allegedly undermining the moderationist argument. Several biblical passages seem upon cursory reading to imply that all wine drinking is prohibited. Anyone committed to the integrity of Scripture should immediately surmise that these observations are in error, for I have shown ample exegetical evidence, drawn from a wide array of passages, which conclusively demonstrates the contrary. Below I will list nine of the more prominent passages employed in the argument against imbibing alcohol. I will provide brief explanatory statements showing that these passages perfectly harmonize with those previously explored.

LEVITICUS 10:8-11

> The LORD then spoke to Aaron, saying, "Do not drink wine or strong drink, neither you nor your sons with you, when you come into the tent of meeting, so that you may not die — it is a perpetual statute throughout your generations — and so as to make a distinction between the holy and profane, and between the unclean and the clean, and so as to teach the sons of Israel all the statutes which the LORD has spoken to them through Moses."

This passage clearly institutes as a "perpetual statute" that members of the Aaronic priesthood should not drink alcoholic beverages when they enter the tabernacle. Nevertheless, against those attempting to use this passage in the present debate, we must note two important qualifications: (1) This prohibition applies only to the priest in the priesthood (Aaron and his sons), and (2) it only forbids the use of alcoholic beverages when the priests are actually engaging in the priestly function. Josephus notes that "as for the priests, [Moses] prescribed to them a double degree of purity" (*Antiquities* 3:12:1). This special purity includes the following: "nor are they permitted to drink wine so long as they wear those garments" (*Antiquities* 3:12:2). The priests only wore their "sacerdotal garments" (*Antiquities* 3:12:2) *while* ministering — "when he enters the holy place" (Ex. 28:2-4, 29), "when he goes in before the LORD" (Ex. 28:30), "when he ministers" (Ex. 28:35), "when they approach the altar to minister in the holy place" (Ex. 28:43).

Apparently God provides this legislation as a safety valve for the priesthood, to prevent any accidental profanation of the tabernacle service. The context seems to demand such an interpretation, for in Leviticus 10:1 we read, "Now Nadab and Abihu, the sons of Aaron, took their respective firepans, and after putting fire in them, placed incense on it and offered strange fire before the LORD, which He had not commanded them."

Verses 2 and 3 give the result of such profaning of the priestly function, and God's reason for such severe punishment:

> And fire came out from the presence of the LORD and consumed them, and they died before the LORD. Then Moses said to Aaron, "It is what the LORD spoke, saying, 'By those who come near Me I will be treated as holy, and

before all the people I will be honored."' So Aaron, therefore,
kept silent.

Nadab and Abihu died because they offered things on
the altar God did not command. Consequently, the priest
must be extremely careful that he follow God's stipulations
in the holy service. Were the priest allowed to drink just
before or during a priestly service, his mind might not
carefully follow God's order of service (Hos. 4:11).
Thus, this passage has nothing to do with us today, since
we are not of the Aaronic priesthood, which has passed away
(Heb. 9 and 10).

Despite these observations, some argue that this
prohibition remains incumbent upon New Testament era
believers because we are "kings and priests" (1 Pet. 2:5, 9;
Rev. 1:6). I will cite the arguments of two representatives
of this strained but popular position. One is prohibitionist
Stephen Reynolds; the other is an abstentionist, Gleason L.
Archer; both are evangelical scholars of great repute. In
Reynolds' case the focus is not on the present passage, but
on Proverbs 31:4-5, which forbids kings to drink. The
manner and assumptions of the arguments of both men are
the same, however.

Referring to Revelation 1:6, which teaches that believers
are "kings and priests," Reynolds states, "It follows, if we
accept this reading, that all Bible believers must be abstainers,
since what was required of kings in the Old Testament is
required of kings under the New." In the next paragraph he
adds, "If ancient kings were warned not to drink intoxicants
lest they forget the law, modern believers who wish to keep
God's law in their heart, should accept this prohibition as
binding on themselves."[1] In a similar vein, and with an
identical spiritual non sequitur, Archer informs us that "this

has implications for the New Testament priesthood of all believers (1 Pet. 2:9) and suggests that they may be seriously handicapped in carrying on the work of soulwinning if they personally indulge in the use of alcohol."[2] This methodology is inappropriate due to a number of problems. A few brief observations will illustrate the spurious nature of such an application of Scripture:

First, if such methodology were proper, both of these provisions (relating to both priests and kings) would witness against our High Priest and King of kings, Jesus Christ. As As I show in Chapter 4, Jesus does partake of wine. This evidence alone exposes the argument's *reductio ad absurdum*.

Second, even in the Old Testament this spiritual truth (that believers are kings and priests) is true. The Old Testament background for both 1 Peter 2:5, 9 and Revelation 1:6 is Exodus 19:6, which reads, "You shall be a kingdom of priests." Yet the Old Testament clearly permits Israelites to manufacture, sell, and drink wine.

Third, both the priestly and kingly prohibitions have implied limitations: The prohibition is in effect *during* the actual exercise of official powers. Leviticus 10:9 particularly commands, "Do not drink wine or strong drink ... *when* you come into the tent of meeting." A similar limitation is strongly implied in the rationale for the prohibition upon kings in Proverbs 31:5: "Lest they drink and forget what is decreed, and pervert the rights of all the afflicted." The perversion of rights could only come about with official sanction, i.e., while acting magisterially or judicially. God prohibits wine-drinking in these limited contexts in order to prevent the frequent corruption of justice brought about by kings who function magisterially while intoxicated (Is. 28:7). Biblical law does not forbid wine to kings permanently and universally (Gen. 14:18-20).

The most we can say of such an argument is that *while in the process* of carrying on the work of soulwinning, the believer as a priest to God should not drink. Or while elders are judicially pursuing church discipline, they are acting as kings and should not imbibe.

Fourth, if we allow such a hermeneutic, what sense could we make of Paul's requirements for the eldership and diaconate? Earlier we saw how the prerequisites specifically exclude only those "addicted to much wine" (1 Tim. 3:8) and those "addicted to wine" (v. 3). Furthermore, how could we understand Paul's "be not drunk with wine"? Why did he not say, "Do not drink wine"?

NUMBERS 6:2-6

> Speak to the sons of Israel, and say to them, "When a man or woman makes a special vow, the vow of a Nazirite, to dedicate himself to the LORD, he shall abstain from wine and strong drink; he shall drink no vinegar, whether made from wine or strong drink, neither shall he drink any grape juice, nor eat fresh or dried grapes. All the days of his separation he shall not eat anything that is produced by the grape vine, from the seeds even to the skin. All the days of his vow of separation no razor shall pass over his head. He shall be holy until the days are fulfilled for which he separated himself to the LORD; he shall let the locks of hair on his head grow long. All the days of his separation to the LORD he shall not go near to a dead person."

Again Scripture here clearly prohibits wine drinking. But just as before, this is a special circumstance irrelevant to our standing and conduct today. This prohibition is a piece of Naziritic legislation that forbade wine only after taking a peculiar, public vow (v. 2). Old covenantal ceremonial actions and vows no longer prevail in the new covenant order (Heb. 8:13).

Furthermore, the Naziritic vow includes avoidance of all grapes (v. 3), cutting of hair (v. 5), and contact with a dead body (v. 6). These limitations go much further than abstentionists and prohibitionists urge. In the final analysis, even this vow was only a *temporary* abstinence: "Then the priest shall wave them for a wave offering before the LORD. It is holy for the priest, together with the breast offered by waving and the thigh offered by lifting up; and afterward the Nazirite may drink wine" (v. 20).

Given its own historical context, Numbers 6 cannot serve as a binding obligation upon believers today. This provides further evidence of the precarious nature of the anti-alcohol moral argument.

JUDGES 13:4

> Now therefore, be careful not to drink wine or strong drink, nor eat any unclean thing.

From time to time anti-alcohol advocates will point to this text as an example of a commendable lifestyle which Scripture encourages. In fact, the call to "be careful not to drink wine or strong drink" is precisely the ethical ideal of abstentionist and prohibitionist Christians.

Unfortunately, though, reading the exhortation *in its context* clearly shows that this is a quite narrowly focused command. The angel of the Lord is speaking to Manoah's wife about her future child, Samson. He will be an unusually gifted judge in Israel with a peculiar ministry:

> And there was a certain man of Zorah, of the family of the Danites, whose name was Manoah; and his wife was barren and had borne no children. Then the angel of the Lord appeared to the woman, and said to her, "Behold now, you

are barren and have borne no children, but you shall conceive and give birth to a son. Now therefore, be careful not to drink wine or strong drink, nor eat any unclean thing. For behold, you shall conceive and give birth to a son, and no razor shall come upon his head, for the boy shall be a Nazirite to God from the womb; and he shall begin to deliver Israel from the hands of the Philistines." (Judg. 13:2-5)

Since this command is quite particular and limited, universally applying it would be a travesty of exposition. Samson was to be a perpetual Nazirite under ceremonial Naziritic proscriptions.

PROVERBS 20:1

Wine is a mocker, strong drink a brawler.
And whoever is intoxicated by it is not wise.

Although not tied to unique circumstance, this verse does not universally prohibit wine drinking. The statement refers to the inebriating potential of wine and strong drink, of which the user must be wary. It warns those who use it immoderately. Note the following observations:

First, the general warning pattern: The warning "wine is a mocker" follows the pattern of 1 Corinthians 8:1, which says that "knowledge makes arrogant." Obviously neither Christian ethics nor a biblical worldview disparage the quest for knowledge as a proper function of rational beings generally, or of Christians specifically. In certain respects wine-consumption and knowledge-acquisition are similar, and bring certain responsibilities with them. That is, each can be used for either good or evil. The point of Proverbs is that wine has the *potential* to mock, just as the point of Paul is that knowledge has the *potential* to make arrogant. Not all who have knowledge are "arrogant." Neither do all who partake of wine become "mockers" or "brawlers."

Second, the particular warning specifics: This warning speaks to the abuse of wine, and not just by analogy. Delitzsch's comments on this passage are very much to the point:

> Wine is a mocker, because he who is intoxicated with it readily scoffs at that which is holy; mead is boisterous . . . because he who is inebriated in his dissolute madness breaks through the limits of morality and propriety. He is unwise who, through wine and the like, i.e. overpowered by it (2 Sam. 13:28), staggers, i.e. he gives himself up to wine to such a degree that he is no longer master of himself.[3]

He adds that the writer is referring to "the passionate slavish desire of wine or for wine." This is why he follows the statement "wine is a mocker, strong drink a brawler" by the comment "he who is *intoxicated* by it is not wise." Thus, the context itself clearly indicates that the *abuse* of wine, the *inordinate* consumption of strong drink is the concern.

Third, the wider warning context: The biblical interpreter must not be selective in his approach to Scripture. We must not divorce particular verses from their wider contexts, nor extract them from the whole system of biblical ethics. I have paraded a mass of evidence before the concerned reader — evidence overwhelmingly supporting the moderationist position. Remember that elsewhere in Scripture we learn that God himself gives us "wine which makes man's heart glad" (Ps. 104:15). Wine is a joyful reward to those obedient to God (Deut. 14:26.). Wine, which in the drunkard's life is a "brawler," is in the poetry of God an emblem of Messianic blessing (Amos 9:13-15). Proverbs 20:1 cannot and must not contradict these positive passages elsewhere.

PROVERBS 21:17

> He who loves pleasure will become a poor man;
> He who loves wine and oil will not become rich.

Prohibitionists widely employ this statement in warning against the end results of wine drinking. Oftentimes opponents of alcoholic beverages point to sociological studies and cultural statistics regarding alcoholism, noting that Proverbs 21:17 warns us of such an outcome. Van Impe's *Alcohol: The Beloved Enemy* and Wilkerson's *Sipping Saints* both weigh in heavily with anecdotal and sociological evidence in this direction. And such ethical breaches and social problems are a concern to moderationists, as well.

But once again, we wrongly apply this verse when promoting total abstinence or prohibition. The verse refers to a constant, inordinate thirst for wine to the neglect of labor and other godly virtues. Notice that the writer does not mention the love of wine alone. He also warns about the love of oil, which was used with perfumes for refreshment from the hot, dry Middle-Eastern sun. Is oil then, an element the righteous must avoid? Obviously not, for God gives man oil (Ps. 104:15). In fact, Proverbs also mentions oil in a good context:

> Oil and perfume make the heart glad,
> So a man's counsel is sweet to his friend. (Prov. 27:9)

Rather, Proverbs 21:17 warns men to keep things in perspective. If the love of money is a root of evil (1 Tim. 6:10), are we then to abstain from all money? Or is it the *love* of money that is the issue?

Actually in its poetic setting, the warning here in Proverbs 21:17 is directed against the party life mentality,

"He who loves pleasure will become a poor man; he who loves wine and oil will not become rich." Note the parallelism: The one who "*loves* wine and oil" is the one who "*loves* pleasure." That is, he is the one who lives a life solely for the pursuit of pleasure, even to the point of riotous abandon. Elsewhere Proverbs describes this type of person similarly:

> For the heavy drinker and the glutton will come to poverty,
> And drowsiness will clothe a man with rags. (Prov. 23:21)

The lifestyle of this person will come to poverty. In 5:11, the writer refers to such party animals: "Woe to those who rise early in the morning that they may pursue strong drink; who stay up late in the evening that wine may inflame them!"

PROVERBS 23:31-32

> Do not look upon the wine when it is red,
> When it sparkles in the cup,
> When it goes down smoothly;
> At the last it bites like a serpent,
> And stings like a viper.

Undoubtedly this passage is one of the most frequently employed texts in the debate over wine drinking. Indeed, prohibitionist Reynolds in his *Alcohol and the Bible* not only opens his major argument (p. 9) with this passage, but closes his book by referring to it (p. 64). He cites this passage over twenty times in his follow up work, *The Biblical Approach to Alcohol.* We may fairly state that, according to Reynolds and those of like persuasion, this passage is the most significant and compelling prohibitionist statement in Scripture. Reynolds comments, "It is the intent of this essay to prove that Proverbs teaches an absolute prohibition against the beverage use of alcohol."[4] Before interpreting the passage, then, it will be helpful to cite some of Reynolds' observations on it.

In a section entitled, "The Absolute Prohibition of Proverbs 23:29-31," we discover the following comments:

> It is true that hyperboles occur in the Bible, but one cannot read Proverbs 23:29-35 without coming to the conclusion that God is speaking of something He loathes as an article for human consumption. There is no suggestion that a good thing which He has given to us to enjoy is in view here. It is viper's poison (verse 32) and the command is not to look on it.[5]

Reynolds then argues from what he deems a parallel situation. He observes that when Lot leaves Sodom, God forbids his looking back upon the city (Gen. 19:17). This is due to the moral evil that infests Sodom. Hence the absolute prohibition by God. Thus, God "also put an absolute prohibition on looking at a certain sort of *yayin* (Prov. 23:31).... The prohibition is absolute, like that of looking at Sodom."[6]

In Reynolds' view the absolute prohibition is here in Proverbs 23 and not at other references to *yayin* because the wine is specifically designated as "red." As I have noted previously, the idea behind this "red" designation is that it is alcoholic, causing redness of eyes and nose when indulged in.[7] Thus, he concludes: "It is puerile to suppose this command is not to be taken seriously and that the prohibition is not absolute. All the prohibitions of Proverbs 23 are absolute."[8]

Reynolds suggests some intriguing arguments based on lexical considerations supporting his view that "red" indicates "alcoholic."[9] And he may well be correct in this observation.

We can concede his point, however, without at all altering the moderationist argument. Note the following observations on the substance of his arguments:

First, we must divorce this passage from its near, far, and ultimate contexts to bear the construction Reynolds places upon it. The *near context* is extremely clear: The warning and admonition specifically apply to *immoderate abusers* of wine:

> 29. Who has woe? Who has sorrow? Who has contentions? Who has complaining? Who has wounds without cause? Who has redness of eyes?
> 30. Those who linger long over wine, those who go to taste mixed wine.
> 31. Do not look on the wine when it is red, when it sparkles in the cup, when it goes down smoothly;
> 32. At the last it bites like a serpent, and stings like a viper.
> 33. Your eyes will see strange things, and your mind will utter perverse things.
> 34. And you will be like one who ties down in the middle of the sea, or like one who lies down on the top of a mast.
> 35. "They struck me, but I did not become ill; they beat me, but I did not know it. When shall I awake? I will seek another drink."

How could a context be any clearer? Here Proverbs specifically and carefully describes the person whom it admonishes. This person exhibits all the emotional, social, and physical characteristics of the drunkard: depression (v. 29a), a contentious spirit (v. 29b), and telltale physical appearance. (v. 29c). Here we have before our view those who "linger long over wine" (v. 30). These drunkards have developed alcohol-induced delusions (v. 33), disorientation (v. 34), and detachment (v. 35a, b). But despite all this, such an addict to wine refuses to give it up (v. 35c).

In his later work, Reynolds considers "strange" my

argument that this passage confronts the drunkard.[10] He asserts that drunkards are not addressed "directly" because they "are not assumed to be teachable."[11] Rather, in this context the writer directs the command "thou," not "this miserable addict."[12]

This is surely a most remarkable claim: Does Scripture give up on those caught up in drunkenness? Are we not to minister to the alcoholic and confront him from Scripture? And why is it just the drunkard who is unteachable; why not those overwhelmed by other addictive sins (such as promiscuity or covetousness)? Does not Proverbs 24:15 directly confront the covetous robber:

> Do not lie in wait, O wicked man, against the dwelling of
> the righteous;
> Do not destroy his resting place.

Actually the Bible does deal directly with drunkards, warning them of their doom: In the rebellious son legislation, the parents obviously attempt rebuke and correction over a period of time (Deut. 21:20). Though it is not successful, nevertheless the attempt is made. In fact, Joel 1:5 expressly addresses the drunkard:

> Awake, drunkards, and weep;
> And wail, all you wine drinkers,
> On account of the sweet wine
> That is cut off from your mouth.

Furthermore, the *broader context* of Proverbs 23 is almost as helpful. Verses 20 through 21 prepare us for the warning of verse 31:

> Do not be with heavy drinkers of wine,
> Or with gluttonous eaters of meat;
> For the heavy drinker and the glutton will come to poverty,
> And drowsiness will clothe a man with rags.

In addition, Reynolds is surely wrong when he forthrightly declares, "the prohibition of Proverbs 23:31 is not properly explained in any other way than *total*."[13] But this no more *universally and absolutely* prohibits wine drinking than verse 4 of the same chapter *universally and absolutely* forbids wealth accumulation:

> Do not weary yourself to gain wealth,
> Cease from your consideration of it.

After all, the Lord grants his obedient people "the power to make wealth" (Deut. 8:18) and promises economic abundance for covenant faithfulness (Deut. 28:1:14; Gen. 13:2; Job 1:1-3). We must understand Proverbs 23:4 contextually. He warns against a *wholesale thirst*, a *driving ambition* to gain wealth, which is much like the alcoholic who gives his life over to a *wholesale thirst* for alcoholic drink.

The *ultimate context* is, of course, the entire Scripture, which clearly does not forbid the moderate partaking of "aged wine" (Is. 25:6), "strong drink" (Deut. 14:26), or "all sorts of wine" (Neh. 5:18). Further, the "gladdening effect" of wine is acceptable, at least to some degree (Ps. 104:15; Eccl. 9:7; 10:19; 2 Sam. 13:28; Esth. 1:10; Zech. 9:15; 10:7; Judg. 9:13).

Second, Reynolds distorts a figure involved in Proverbs 23:32. The text does not say, "It is a viper's poison."[14] Rather, it warns, "at the last it bites *like* a serpent, and stings *like* an adder." A world of difference separates reality ("is") and analogy ("is like"). It is only "at the last," after "lingering long," that wine becomes harmful "like" a viper. The *abuse* of wine is in view here, not the *use*.

In this respect it is somewhat similar to Isaiah 1:10-14, which reads:

Hear the word of the Lord, you rulers of Sodom;
Give ear to the instruction of our God, you people of Gomorrah.
"What are your multiplied sacrifices to Me?" says the Lord.
"I have had enough of burnt offerings of rams,
And the fat of fed cattle.
And I take no pleasure in the blood of bulls, lambs, or goats.
When you come to appear before Me,
Who requires of you this trampling of My courts?
Bring your worthless offerings no longer.
Incense is an abomination to Me.
New moon and sabbath, the calling of assemblies —
I cannot endure iniquity and the solemn assembly.
I hate your new moon festivals and your appointed feasts,
They have become a burden to Me. I am weary of bearing them."

Under the particular circumstances, the otherwise God-ordained sacrifices, offerings, incense, assemblies, and feasts are an unendurable burden to the Lord (vv. 13-14). Obviously the context must inform us *why* God hates these good things. And it does: The rulers of Israel are living like those of Sodom, the people like those of Gomorrah (v. 10). Their hands are "covered with blood" (v. 15). In short, at this time Israel is a "sinful nation, a people weighed down with iniquity, offspring of evildoers, sons who act corruptly!" (v. 4). God does not accept the worship of the hypocrite and the rebel.

Third, Reynolds' particular illustration destroys his own argument. A careful reading of Genesis 19 indicates the limited nature of the prohibition to look upon Sodom and Gomorrah. God forbids Lot and his family to look back (v. 17) *while* God's wrath is falling upon those cities. Lot's wife looks back at that moment, and she dies (v. 26). But Abraham looks down upon the cities shortly *after* the judgment and lives (vv. 27-28). Likewise it is with the long-lingering alcoholic (Prov. 23:30), one who refuses moderation (v. 35) — wisdom forbids *his* looking upon wine.

Fourth, although Reynolds may be correct in asserting that the reference to "red" in Proverbs 23:31 indicates the wine's alcoholic content, it is simply not true that "there was no other word in the ancient languages in which the Bible was written for alcoholic beverages."[15] Reynolds admits differing with the consensus of Bible translations over this point. As I point out in chapter 3, lexicographers affirm what Reynolds denies: *oinos*, *shekar*, and other terms *do in fact* refer to alcoholic wine. And if Reynolds is correct when he asserts that the phrase in Proverbs 23:31 is the only phrase that refers to alcohol, then this one verse becomes the *only* verse in all of Scripture that warns of alcohol abuse!

ISAIAH 5:21-22

> Woe to those who are wise in their own eyes,
> And clever in their own sight!
> Woe to those who are heroes in drinking wine,
> And valiant men in mixing strong drink.

This passage calls down woes upon "heroes in drinking wine." And rightly so. But clearly this does not *universally* condemn all wine drinking. This should be evident for a number of reasons:

First, as we have seen, abundant evidence from Scripture shows that wine may be consumed in a righteous manner and by righteous men — including even the Son of God. And Scripture does not contradict Scripture.

Second, we find these verses set in a larger judgment context, where the prophet condemns other normally acceptable practices. For instance, verse 8 calls down woe upon those who "join house to house." Is multiplying real

estate holdings *always* sinful? In verse 12 we learn that the
Jews are attending banquets where music is produced "by
lyre and harp, tambourine and flute." Are public festivities
involving music *necessarily* evil?

Third, the immediate context already suggests the
moderationist's interpretation:

> Woe to those who rise early in the morning that they may
> pursue strong drink;
> Who stay up late in the evening that wine may inflame them!
> (Is. 5:11)

Note that these "rise early" to "pursue strong drink";
they "stay up late in the evening" so that "wine may *inflame*
them." These men are *not* moderate drinkers! In fact, Isaiah
condemns them because they "drag iniquity with the cords
of falsehood" (v. 18) and "call evil good and good evil" (v.
19). These men are "wise in their own eyes" (v. 20) and
"justify the wicked for a bribe" (v. 23). Immediately before
the condemnation of those who justify the wicked by
accepting bribes (v. 23) we read our verse about "heroes in
drinking wine" (vv. 21-22). What could be more clear?

Consequently, verses 21 and 22 refer to an *abuse* of wine
by *judges* (v. 23). J. A. Alexander notes that "the tone of this
verse is sarcastic, from its using terms which express not
only strength but courage and heroic spirit, in application to
exploits of drunkenness."[16]

JEREMIAH 35:6

> But they said, "We will not drink wine, for Jonadab, the son
> of Rechab, our father, commanded us, saying, 'You shall not
> drink wine, you or your sons, forever.'"

From time to time those who forbid wine drinking will

point to this episode in Scripture as a noble example of a fitting testimony to abstinence. Once again, though, this does not stand as a universal, divine obligation to abstinence from alcohol.

First, note that this is a *human* command which Jonadab gives to his sons (vv. 5, 6, 8). This testimonial carries with it no "thus saith the Lord." Rather it is a family practice that passes down by human authority through the line of this singular family. We must not universalize testimonies of individual families — even those that appear very noble — otherwise we would all dedicate our children to temple service, as did Samuel's mother (1 Sam. 1:11, 20-22) and commit our children to Naziritic holiness, as did Samson's mother (Judg. 13:5).

Second, it also forbids the owning of a house (vv. 7, 9). Obviously, owning a home is not sinful. In fact, the Lord Jesus Christ himself promises blessings of houses to his faithful followers: "Truly I say to you, there is no one who has left house or brothers or sisters or mother or father or children or farms, for My sake and for the gospel's sake, but that he shall receive a hundred times as much now in the present age, houses and brothers and sisters and mothers and children and farms, along with persecutions; and in the age to come, eternal life" (Mark 10:29-30).

Third, the context of this command implies that this was a form of prophetic theater. That is, this obligation serves as a prophecy acted out against sinful conditions. For instance, Hosea lives out prophetic theater when God commands him to marry a harlot (Hos. 1:2; 3:1) as a symbolic portrayal of God's love for unfaithful, idolatrous Israel (Hos. 1:2, 4-11). Here in Jeremiah 35 the sons of Jonadab portray a spiritual truth by keeping this vow. By obeying this obviously *unnecessary* and *unreasonable* command of their father, they serve as a testimony against faithless Israel for her refusal to obey God's *good* and *reasonable* law (Jer. 35:12-19).

HOSEA 7:5

> On the day of our king, the princes became sick with the heat of wine;
> He stretched out his hand with scoffers.

Reynolds uses this passage to forcefully illustrate the dangerous nature of alcoholic wine. In fact, his chapter title is "Hosea 7:5 and the Question of the Poisonous Nature of Wine When It Is Alcoholic."[17] He attempts an interesting lexical argument to prove that the word usually translated "heat" should better be translated "poison":

> The question still remains whether *chamath* is properly to be translated heat, anger, or poison. *Chemah* from which it is derived may have any one of these meanings, the context being used to determine which meaning is correct in any particular case.
>
> Here the reader must choose between — the heat of wine makes sick, the anger or wrath of wine makes sick, or the poison of wine makes sick. Poison regularly makes the one who takes it sick. Heat and anger may sometimes make the person who is affected by them sick, but not regularly. Therefore poison is to be preferred.
>
> We must notice that the Bible does not say that this poison is something other than alcohol which malicious people have added to the king's wine. It is the poison *of* wine, that is the poison of alcohol, the poison in grape juice which has fermented.
>
> We already have a reference in Proverbs 23:32 to alcoholic wine's being like the bite of a poisonous snake. When adequately translated, Hosea 7:5 is a second reference to the poison of (alcoholic) wine.[18]

In response, note that though Reynolds prefers the

translation "poison," *no modern translation committee does.* And for good reason: The context all around it crackles with flames. Consider the surrounding context and note how nicely "heat" fits in the passage:

> They are all adulterers
> Like an *oven heated* by the baker,
> Who ceases to stir up the *fire*
> From the kneading of the dough until it is leavened.
> On the day of our king, the princes became sick with the *heat* of wine;
> He stretched out his hand with scoffers,
> For their hearts are like an *oven*
> As they approach their plotting;
> Their anger *smolders* all night,
> In the morning it *burns* like a *flaming fire.*
> All of them are *hot* like an *oven,*
> And they consume their rulers;
> All their kings have fallen.
> None of them calls on Me. (Hos. 7:4-7, emphases mine)

Furthermore, the imagery Hosea presents is of rulers who are *drunk* on wine. They are "sick with ... wine," which is a familiar problem with those who drink *too much* of it (Is. 19:14; 28:8; Jer. 25:27; 48:26). This *abuse* of wine by men in positions of authority is a common problem that the prophets confront — and which explains Proverbs 31:4-5 — as we may discern from a several references (Is. 5:22-23; 19:14; 28:7; 56:12).

CONCLUSION

In Chapters 2 through 5, I survey evidence presenting a balanced approach to the many scriptural statements expressly dealing with alcoholic beverages. As a "People of the Book," Christians must lay aside all preconceptions and carefully consider the express teachings of the Bible on this issue. As I point out in Chapter 1 the starting point and guiding principle of Christian theistic ethics is the self-validating and authoritative Word of God. The Scripture must be the believer's final arbiter in moral discourse rather than emotional, pragmatic, cultural, or intuitive considerations.

The above chapters clearly show that drunkenness, alcohol dependency, and alcohol abuse are indeed grave sins leading to social, moral, spiritual, and economic degradation. God's holy Word expressly condemns these forms of abuse. Yet we commit the informal logical fallacy of hasty generalization when we leap from a scriptural condemnation of alcohol *abuse* to conclude that the *use* of alcohol is evil. Fermented wines of all sorts play a significant role in the lives of God's people in both Old and New Testament times.

In support of mandatory total abstinence, prohibitionist Henry Morris argues that "it is significant that nowhere does the Bible actually endorse the drinking of wine or other intoxicating drinks."[19] This statement is patently mistaken and demonstrates the all-too-frequent tendency among evangelicals to lightly review the scriptural data and proceed on intuitive feelings or some other criteria. *Yayin* ("wine"), which Morris himself concedes is a fermented beverage,[20] is a gift righteous men exchange in godly circumstances (Gen. 14:18-20). It is an offering God requires in worship (Ex. 29:38, 40), is a blessing of God (Ps. 104:14-15), and symbolizes Messianic blessings (Is. 25:6). In fact, God removes it as an aspect of covenantal curse (Deut. 28:39). Furthermore, even our Lord Jesus Christ drank wine (Luke 7:33-34), produced it through miraculous intervention (John 2:1-10), and instituted the Lord's Supper with it (Matt. 26:29).

Thus, as Heinrich Seeseman observes, "Wine is very significant in Palestine," and in the Old Testament "abstinence from wine ... is rare." Although the Old

Testament does not enjoin mandatory total abstinence, nevertheless, notes Seeseman, "there are many warnings against overindulgence."[21]

   We cannot reasonably argue that wine — any kind of wine, whether new wine, sweet wine, or aged strong drink — is universally prohibited in Scripture. Wine, to be sure, can be and is abused just as other good gifts from God can be and are abused — e.g., sex (Rom. 13:13), food (Prov. 23:20-21), and wealth (1 Tim. 6:9-11). Yet God intends sex (Heb. 13:4), food (Ps. 104:14- 15), and wealth (Job 42:10-17) to be good blessings; we must employ them in faith and according to the directives of biblical law.

CHAPTER 6

BIBLE TEACHING ON CHRISTIAN LIBERTY

As I show in Chapter 1, drunkenness is a heinous sin in the sight of God. Scripture dogmatically and vividly denounces alcohol abuse in a great number of ways. Despite this observation, Scripture not only *condones* alcoholic beverages but it expressly *allows* them for God's people. This is quite contrary to prohibitionist arguments.

A question now arises: In light of the *present* danger of alcohol abuse does Christian *prudence* encourage permanent abstinence from alcoholic beverages *for the sake of others*? This argument distinguishes the abstentionist position from the prohibitionist one. The difference between the two positions is that of "love" versus "law." Abstentionists argue their position on the basis of love for those around us whom we might lead astray, whereas prohibitionists present a case for specific biblical prohibition across the board. The contrast is that between voluntary total abstinence and mandatory total prohibition.

This is no mere academic question either. It is a matter of far-reaching practical and theological importance. Is the Christian under obligation to alter his behavior, which in itself is not sinful, for the sake of others? And if so, under what circumstances? And to what degree? And for how long?

Fortunately, the Scripture addresses this very issue in detail in two forceful passages of the New Testament: Romans 14 and 1 Corinthians 8-10.

INTRODUCTION TO ROMANS 14

In this part of our study I will focus on the Romans 14 passage rather than 1 Corinthians 8-10. I do this for several reasons:

1. To study both would require much more space than really necessary to answer the question. I will employ the Romans 14 passage as the shorter and more concise of the two.

2. The two passages are similar enough in their major principles and argumentative thrust that such a combined study would not only be overly long but also redundant. Where necessary I will incorporate into my Romans 14 exposition specific references to distinctive statements from 1 Corinthians.

3. Romans 14, unlike the 1 Corinthians passage, refers particularly and explicitly to the exact issue at hand: wine drinking (Rom. 14:17, 21). Some even consider it to be the *locus classicus* on the issue.[1]

4. Unlike the Romans 14 passage, 1 Corinthians 8-10 introduces the matter from a significantly different angle. When Paul writes Corinth he presents the issue of abstinence from foods offered to idols. This is not a directly relevant problem for modern Western Christians.

The church at Rome had specific, identifiable, real-life problems involving religious scruples resulting in inner-church discord. Sanday observes that three specific issues seem to be plaguing the church and that Paul speaks to these:

There appears to have been a party in the Church at Rome

which had adopted certain ascetic practices over and above the common rule of Christianity. We gather that they abstained altogether from flesh and wine, and that they ... made a point of observing certain days with peculiar sanctity.[2]

The problems at Rome revolve around eating meat (versus vegetarianism), drinking wine (versus abstinence), and observing days (versus religious liberty).

Furthermore, we must understand the broader context of this section of Romans. In Romans 14 Paul is clarifying two general biblical principles. First, he is urging the Roman Christians in a very practical way to "prove what the will of God is" regarding Christians' differing capacities (Rom. 12:1-6). Second, in so doing he directs them to apply agape love, which is the summary of the holy law of God (Matt. 22:36-40; Rom. 13:8-10; Gal. 5:14; James 2:8). Thus, the passage explains how, in light of the obvious problems at Rome, to "put on the Lord Jesus Christ, and make no provision for the flesh in regard to its lusts" (Rom. 13:14). The following three sections will provide a verse-by-verse exposition of this important passage.

"WEAK" AND "STRONG" BELIEVERS

Romans 14:1: Now accept the one who is weak in faith, but not for the purpose of passing judgment on his opinions.

By employing the imperative mood, Paul commands the strong believer to accept the one who is weak in faith. Although some similarities exist between the material of Romans 14 (especially vv. 2-3, 6) and that of Galatians 4:10ff and Colossians 2:16-17, 20-23, a very basic difference arises, as well. In Galatia and Colossae the problem of foods and days is *heretical*, affecting the Christian gospel at its heart.

Consequently, the apostle severely rebukes and vehemently condemns their views (Gal. 1:6-9; 33; 4:11, 20; 5:4; and Col. 2:1-8, 14-23). On the other hand, in Romans the problem exposes spiritual *weakness* and intellectual *confusion*. The Romans are not guilty of distorting theological truth in such a way as to incorporate alien doctrine into the very foundation of Christian salvation.

The word Paul employs to designate one party as "weak" is the Greek word *astheneo*. This word literally refers to a physical ailment. The Arndt-Gingrich lexicon notes here the word figuratively denotes religious and moral weakness — the "weak" were "over-scrupulous."[3] Paul does not leave this weakness unspecified; rather he qualifies it by the dative of realm: *pistei*, "faith." The realm of the particular weakness is the realm of faith. Thayer notes that Romans 14:1 (and 1 Cor. 8:9) indicates that these weak ones are "doubtful about things lawful and unlawful to a Christian." The term "weak" describes one "who is weak (in his feelings and conviction about things lawful)."[4] Significantly, Paul separates the two groups into the categories of "weak" and "strong" in terms of their faith. Paul himself is in the camp of the "strong" (Rom. 15:1).

Paul urges the strong to "receive" the weak. The customary word used for "receive" in the Greek is *lambano*. Here, however, we find *proslambano*. By adding the preposition *pros* to the verb stem, Paul strongly emphasizes his statement, as if to say, "You must truly and fully receive the weak into your fellowship!"[5] We see how open their reception must be: The strong are not to receive them "for the purpose of passing judgments" on their (weak) "opinions." That is, they must *not* receive the weak hoping to corner them and criticize their weakness on these matters (foods, days, and wine).[6]

> **Romans 14:2-3**: One man has faith that he may eat all things, but he who is weak eats vegetables only. Let not him who eats regard with contempt him who does not eat, and let not him who does not eat judge him who eats, for God has accepted him.

In verse 2, Paul specifies the first area of religious scrupulosity he will address. The one who cannot eat meat is the *weak* one in the context. The strong one understands that God allows the eating of "all things." Paul touches on this matter in other contexts, clearly allowing consumption of meat (1 Tim. 4:3). (As someone satirically put it: "If God had not intended for us to eat animals, why did he make them out of meat?")

Verse 3 enjoins both parties with the command to mutual concern. The strong must not "despise, disdain,"[7] "make of no account"[8] the one who abstains from certain foods (i.e., meat). But here Paul also commands the *weak* to express agape love (a point we often overlook): The weak brother is not to "censoriously judge,"[9] or "criticize, find fault with"[10] the strong. If the weak one does so, he is censuring one fully accepted by God in the matter. John Murray makes a pertinent comment on this verse: "It is iniquity for us to condemn what God approves. By so doing we presume to be holier than God."[11]

> **Romans 14:4**: Who are you to judge the servant of another? To his own master he stands or falls, and stand he will, for the Lord is able to make him stand.

This continues the command to the weak regarding their treatment of the strong.[12] While Scripture is explicit that Christians ought to confront and rebuke sin in fellow believers,[13] Paul makes it clear that weaker Christians should not rebuke a stronger Christian for something that it is not in fact a sin. He makes his point by noting what Murray calls "the impropriety of intermeddling in the domestic affairs of other people."[14] Sanday observes that "the Apostle indignantly challenges his [the weak Christian's] right to judge. That right belongs to another tribunal, before which the conduct of the stronger Christian will not be condemned but approved and upheld."[15]

Thus Paul begins at this point to establish the doctrine that the Westminster Confession of Faith terms "Christian liberty" (WCF 20). No man can bind the conscience of another on an issue that is not condemned by Scripture either expressly or implicitly. Significantly, Paul directs both the weak *and* the strong — and not just the strong, as some today seem to expect. R.C.H. Lenski observes that "the weak often do more harm in the church than the strong."[16]

> **Romans 14:5**: One man regards one day above another, another regards every day alike. Let each man be fully convinced in his own mind.

Paul here begins addressing another source of actual contention in the church at Rome: religious observance of various holy days. He recognizes that some at Rome are convinced that the Lord has specified numerous religious days to be observed with special devotion.

Paul obviously sides with those who do *not* observe various days.[17] If God still demands observing of the various religious holy days and festivals of the Old Testament era,[18] then not observing them would be disobedience to a direct command of God. Such a practice would not be a matter of "weakness" or "strength," because it would not be an issue of Christian liberty at all. It would be a willful sin and therefore subject to both divine rebuke and ecclesiastical censure, in that "sin is lawlessness" (1 John 3:4). Paul would never leave an issue such as that to one's individual discretion. Paul is urging individual responsibility to live up to one's convictions (v. 23).

> **Romans 14:6-12:** He who observes the day, observes it for the Lord, and he who eats, does so for the Lord, for he gives thanks to God; and he who eats not, for the Lord he does not eat, and gives thanks to God. For not one of us lives for himself, and not one dies for himself, for if we live, we live for the Lord, or if we die, we die for the Lord; therefore whether we live or die, we are the Lord's. For to this end Christ died and lived again, that He might be Lord both of the dead and of the living. But you, why do you judge your brother? Or you again, why do you regard your brother with contempt? For we shall all stand before the judgment seat of God. For it is written, "As I live, says the Lord, every knee shall bow to me, and every tongue shall give praise to God."

At this point Paul again emphasizes that there is but one Lord who judges a man's conscience. He adds that each person is individually obligated only to God's will in terms of basic convictions. The Christian's obligation is not to the will of the many round about him but to the one Lord above them; he and he alone is the judge of all men.

NATURE OF THE "STUMBLING BLOCK"

Believers are quite familiar with the principle of a "stumbling block" in the Christian walk. Unfortunately, the actual *nature* of this concept is not as widely known and understood. At this juncture I will analytically consider the biblical data relative to the stumbling block.

> **Romans 14:13:** Therefore let us not judge one another anymore, but rather determine this — not to put an obstacle or a stumbling block in a brother's way.

This is perhaps the most crucial verse in the whole discussion of Christian liberty. Based on the obligations of Christians to one another, Paul here shifts his focus from a discussion of internal heartfelt attitudes and publicly expressed verbalizations (as discussed in verses 1 through 12) to actual behavior arising out of thoughts and words.

Paul is now beginning to address the strong in this passage. Note the following proofs of this:

1. He speaks in the first person in this address in verse 13: "Let *us* not judge." Paul expressly declares himself in the camp of the strong: "Now we who are strong ought to bear the weaknesses of those without strength and not just please ourselves" (Rom. 15:1).

2. Logically it is more likely that the weak were the ones more in danger of "stumbling" — by the very nature of their being weak. Strength implies stability (Ps. 30:7; Prov. 18:10; Is. 26:1), weakness instability (Lev. 26:36; Ezek. 21:7).

3. Here the danger of a stumbling block refers to the convictions against eating certain foods (vv. 14, 21, 23). The strong would not have such scruples, since Scripture everywhere allows the consuming of meat. For instance, the whole sacrificial system implies not only animal death but meat eating (Ex. 12:3-9).

4. The moral stumbling results in "destruction" (v. 15), which suggests better the fragility of the "weak."

Of utmost importance to the present issue is our determining what Paul means when he exhorts the strong "not to put an obstacle or a stumbling block in a brother's way" (v. 13). To properly understand this exhortation requires a brief word study of the Greek words employed here: *proskomma* ("stumbling block") and *skandalon* ("obstacle"). As the authoritative *Theological Dictionary of the New Testament* observes:

In Paul's pastoral handling of the debate between the strong and the weak in Corinth ... and Rome ... the words *skandalon*, *skandalizomai* [the verbal form of the former noun], *proskomma, proskopto* [the verbal form of the preceding noun] ... are the crucial catchwords.[19]

Proskomma. Popular discussion of this important Romans 14 passage too often obscures the concept of "stumbling block." Many assume this refers to a matter that perturbs, disquiets, or annoys a fellow believer. However, *proskomma* has far stronger connotations than these words suggest.

In the Greek version of the Hebrew Old Testament (the Septuagint), *proskomma* occurs quite frequently. In Exodus 23:33, for instance, God warns Israel that serving false gods would be a "snare" (*proskomma*) to her. Obviously then, *proskomma* leads directly into great sin.

In Isaiah 8:14-15 the prophet warns Israel that rejecting Christ, who should be a sanctuary for her, would cause Christ to become a "stone of stumbling" for her. Because Israel would reject her savior, Christ would cause her to "fall and be broken," i.e., to be brought to utter ruin. Our theology informs us that those who "stumble" (*proskopto*) at Christ fall into absolutely devastating and utter ruin — i.e., into hell itself (Matt. 25:40-41; Rev. 14:11). Consequently, the *Theological Dictionary of the New Testament* notes the serious consequences of *proskomma* as an obstacle: "it is thus easy to see how *proskomma* ... can be used in the sense of 'personified destruction.'"[20]

In Romans 9:32, 1 Peter 2:8, and 1 Corinthians 1:23 the New Testament explicitly designates Jesus as Israel's "stone of stumbling" by referring to Isaiah 8:14. The prophetic utterances concerning Israel's apostasy and ruin fall from the lips of the Lord himself, thereby testifying to the gravity of "stumbling" over him (Matt. 8:12; 21:43-44; 23:32-24:2).[21] Israel's rejecting the "chief corner stone" results in her being broken to pieces and scattered like dust (Luke 20:17-18). Israel's "stumbling" and her subsequent destruction are inseparably connected.

Thus, Thayer's lexicon defines *proskomma* as follows: "stumbling block, i.e. an obstacle in the way which if one strike his foot against he necessarily stumbles or falls ... i.e. by which it [the soul] is impelled to sin."[22] Consequently then, "to put a stumbling block in one's way" is "to furnish one an occasion for sinning."[23] The *Theological Dictionary of the New Testament* notes that in Romans 14 and 1 Corinthians 8 a *proskomma* is a "hindrance to faith" in that it is a "cause of spiritual ruin." Thus, "at issue in the question of *proskomma* are ultimate decisions, conscience and faith, sin and perdition"[24] and not simple matters of annoyance or irritation.

Skandalon. This noun and its verbal form occur frequently in the Septuagint. According to the *Theological Dictionary of the New Testament,* in the Septuagint its main Old Testament meanings are "occasion of guilt" and "cause of destruction."[25] Very simply it means, "cause of ruin."[26]

Skandalon frequently appears in the New Testament. The Arndt-Gingrich lexicon defines it as follows: "1. trap. 2. temptation to sin, enticement to apostasy, false belief, etc."[27] Thayer adds, "a. properly, the moveable stick or [trigger] of a trap, trap-sack.... b. metaphorically any person or thing by which one is ('entrapped') drawn into error or sin."[28] Thus, "as in the OT it is the cause of both transgression and destruction."[29]

The notion that the *skandalon* is the causal factor of actual transgression is vital to this word. Consequently, "*ta skandala* are those who seduce into breaking the Law [in the

Septuagint usage]. In the NT interpretation they are those who lead into sin and apostasy."[30]

In summary, when Paul enjoins the strong's concern for the weak, he encourages them to be careful that they not entice or tempt a weak believer into *overtly sinful behavior*. He does not teach that Christians must avoid perturbing other Christians. The words he employs here are much too strong for such a light meaning.

CONDUCT OF CHRISTIAN LIBERTY

In this section Paul closes in on the actual conduct of Christian liberty in light of the mix of the weak and strong brethren and the nature of the stumbling block.

> **Romans 14:14**: I know and am convinced in the Lord Jesus that nothing is unclean in itself; but to him who thinks anything to be unclean, to him it is unclean.

Very emphatically Paul sides with the strong over against the weak concerning the eating of foods (v. 2). When Paul claims, "I know and am convinced," he is speaking with clear, apostolic conviction. He is not saying, "Personally, it is my opinion in this case that probably...." He is resolutely convinced. Furthermore, he insists that his conviction in this matter derives from the Lord himself, not from social considerations, nor from human deliberation. He will allow no debate on this principle; it is not a culturally relative ethical standard. He is convinced "in the Lord Jesus."

The apostle affirms that "nothing is unclean in itself." Murray well sums up the intent of Paul's statement in this regard:

> This principle is the refutation of all prohibitionism which lays the responsibility for wrong at the door of things rather

than at man's heart. The basic evil of this ethic is that it makes God the Creator responsible and involves both blasphemy and the attempt to alleviate human responsibility for wrong.[31]

Paul's convictions are in keeping with a biblical worldview, which sees the creation itself as good, and sin as a moral factor stirring in the fallen will of man (Matt. 15:10-20). He rejects Platonic, neo-Platonic, and Gnostic conceptions of sin as an element lodged in the material realm.

While on this matter, we should note that some prohibitionists attempt to sidestep the issue by averring that wine is not a creation of God, but of man. Reynolds provides a classic case in point: "Fermented beverages would not occur without man's entering into the process. (Man must press the grapes before the yeast turns the grape sugar into alcohol.)"[32] But here an uneasy feeling arises that he is creating evidence *ex nihilo* — in order to "prove" a point. Many problems plague observations of this nature.

To begin, the statement is not scientifically accurate (see discussion in Chapter 3). The authoritative *Encyclopedia of Alcoholism* notes that "fermentation can occur naturally, with airborne yeasts converting any sugary mash into ethyl alcohol and carbon dioxide."[33] Even abstentionist documents admit this, as we see in the alcohol study released by the Reformed Presbyterian Church, Evangelical Synod: "The process of fermentation is a splitting up of sugar molecules by the action of yeast. The yeast cells are common in nature, and fermentation takes place automatically if conditions are right."[34]

A question naturally arises from the midst of such prohibitionist concerns: Should men *not* extract grape juice at all — since it naturally (and dangerously) tends to ferment? In addition, the text we are especially considering includes wine in its discussion of a food that is in itself a "good thing" (Rom. 14:16, 20). Finally, in such a position what becomes of Paul's statement here that "nothing is unclean of itself" (v. 14)? And of Jesus' teaching in Mark 7:14-23, which speaks similarly.

Turning once again to the text before us, we admit that eating of perfectly good food *can* be sinful — given the proper moral context. For instance, if someone is convinced in his heart that partaking of certain foods is sinful in the sight of God (as Seventh-Day Adventists believe about pork), then *for him* to willfully partake *against* his basic convictions *is* sin. If he believes deeply within his heart that eating a certain food item is forbidden by God, and yet he then partakes of that item despite his spiritual moral convictions, he is in willful rebellion against God (vv. 20, 23).

> **Romans 14:15**: For if because of food your brother is hurt, you are no longer walking according to love. Do not destroy with your food him for whom Christ died.

How can the strong Christian's eating food "hurt" the brother? What is Paul actually warning against here? The Arndt-Gingrich lexicon defines the verb *lupeo* (in the verbal form found here) as follows: "be sad, be distressed, grieve" or "injure, damage."[35] The idea of "distress" or "injury" would fit best here in light of the preceding context in verse 13 (see previous discussion of "stumbling block"). Also, Paul later deems the effect of the strong Christian's eating as involving a "tearing down" (v. 20).

The following context thus confirms the serious nature of this "hurt" (see especially vv. 20-23). The "hurt" is not simply annoyance, perturbation, or disappointment aroused in the weak. Murray again offers excellent commentary on Paul's train of thought:

> The grief befalling the weak is morally and religiously destructive. The sin committed, therefore, is of a grievous character and the grief can be nothing less than the vexation of conscience that afflicts a believer when he violates conscience and does what he esteems to be disloyalty to Christ.[36]

The "hurt" is the pang of a guilty conscience that results from the weak Christian's being enticed into sin (or what he deems to be sin) by the behavior of the strong. The strong believer in such a situation causes the weaker brother to sin against his conscience; because of that, he is not walking "according to love."

Paul so structures verse 15 as to suggest the remnants of a *parallelismus membrorum*, a common poetic device in Hebraic literature. The parallelism in this case has affinities with a distich line composing a synonymous parallelism pattern. Note how the essential concepts of two parts of the thought "rhyme" in their meaning:

1. Because of your food ... your brother ... is hurt.

2. With your food ... the one for whom Christ died ... do not destroy.

Whether or not the above pattern is a remnant of a formal Hebraic parallelism as suggested, obviously the words "hurt" (*lupeo*) and "destroy" (*appollumi*) mutually explain each other.[37] Consequently, the hurt that the stronger brother causes in the weaker is equivalent to his being destroyed.

Appollumi is a very strong word that means to "ruin, destroy,"[38] "to put out of the way entirely, abolish, put an end to, ruin ... render useless."[39] Of the specific verse under consideration, lexicographers and commentators generally agree that it means "by one's conduct to cause another to lose eternal salvation."[40]

Theologian Charles Hodge explains this verse:

Believers (the elect) are constantly spoken of as in danger
of perdition. They are saved only if they continue steadfast
unto the end. If they apostatize, they perish. If the Scriptures
tell the people of God what is the tendency of their sins, as
to themselves, they may tell them what is the tendency of
such sins as to others.[41]

Simply put, Paul is here warning about the outcome of
enticing the weaker brother into sinning against his
conscience — which will bring God's judgment. Although
no true believer can lose his unmerited, sovereignly bestowed
salvation, Paul's injunction reflects the numerous biblical
warnings about apostasy. Clearly, it is a very serious matter
that the strong not behave in such a way as to lead the weaker
Christian into sinning against his conscience.

> **Romans 14:16-17**: Therefore do not let what is for you a
> good thing be spoken of as evil; for the kingdom of God is
> not eating and drinking, but righteousness and peace and
> joy in the Holy Spirit.

The "therefore" draws a conclusion to Paul's statements
in verses 13 through 15 concerning the conduct of the strong.
The "good thing" refers to the strong one's sure knowledge
of Christian liberty. Because of the weaker believers who
deem it wrong to eat or drink certain things, and because the
strong can tempt them to sin against the dictates of their
conscience, Paul emphasizes that the strong one must not
abuse his strength by actually leading weaker believers to sin
against their consciences. If he does so, his Christian liberty
will be the subject of ridicule and scorn.

> **Romans 14:18-19**: For he who in this way serves Christ is
> acceptable to God and approved by men. So then let us
> pursue the things which make for peace and the building up
> of one another.

Paul teaches that the strong who use their liberty wisely, carefully, and lovingly not only please God but will be approved in the sight of men. In the preceding verses the liberty abuser causes shame among men because he entices weaker believers into sin against their consciences (v. 16). The two effects are opposites: The careless abuser of the Christian liberty ideal receives ridicule; the wise user of Christian liberty is approved by men. Consequently, the strong must actively seek peace and edification among all believers.

We should recall the particular problems of this church in order to gain the proper perspective on this statement. From verses 1, 3, 4, 10, and 13 obviously two camps — the strong and the weak — are warring over religious scruples. Rather than edifying each other, they pass judgment, disapprove, and hold each other up to contempt.

> **Romans 14:20**: Do not tear down the work of God for the sake of food. All things indeed are clean, but they are evil for the man who eats and gives offense.

The primary concern of the kingdom of God is not eating and drinking, but essential spiritual qualities that govern all things, including eating and drinking (v. 17). Consequently, the strong Christian must be careful not to abuse his liberty. If his actions cause weak believers to stumble into sin (v. 13) so as to be deeply grieved for their rebellion (v. 15), then the strong one is tearing down the "work of God," the weak believer. This is especially serious if the weak dwells in his sin against his own conscience. This is tantamount to apostasy (v. 15).

Paul's statement "they are evil for the man who eats and gives offense" (v. 20) is vitally important. It teaches that when a weaker brother is finally lured into eating against his conscience, he "offends" (*proskomatta*) — he sins against his own conscience and thus against what he believes to be the very will of God. He is then in open rebellion against God.

> **Romans 14:21**: It is good not to eat meat or to drink wine or to do anything by which your brother stumbles.

Before considering the exegesis of this verse, I must make a brief textual comment. The *King James Version* adds to this verse the following words: "or is offended, or is made weak." The better Greek manuscripts, however, omit these. Eminent Greek scholar Bruce M. Metzger, in his important *A Textual Commentary on the Greek New Testament*, suggests that these additional words, which occur in a few ancient manuscripts, were a later copyist's expansion of the text.[42]

In keeping with the available manuscript evidence and the prevailing textual critical theory, the United Bible Societies' fourth edition of *The Greek New Testament* omits the words from the text and relegates them to a footnote, indicating their dubious authenticity. The twenty-third edition of Nestle's *Novum Testamentum Graece* does so also. The R.V.G. Tasker *Greek New Testament* omits them without so much as a comment. Versions that follow suit include the *New American Standard Bible*, *American Standard Version*, *New International Version*, *Revised Standard Version*, *Phillips*, *New English Bible*, and *Today's English Version*. Thus, I will not consider them as authentic to the original text.

Along with Romans 14:13 and 1 Corinthians 8:13 this verse is one of the more misunderstood verses in the debate over Christian liberty. Some would wrongly understand this verse to mean that all Christians everywhere and under all circumstances are obligated by Holy Writ to maintain a life of total abstinence. But we can see that this is patently false by a quick reading of the text. Do the same people insist upon total abstinence from *meat* based on the text? Paul does say, after all: "It is good not to eat meat or drink wine."

Others who call for total abstinence argue in the following manner: "In light of the abuse of alcohol in present American culture the Christian should abstain from alcoholic beverages. After all, meat is not abused in America." This argument, of course, overlooks the ridicule in vogue by the socialist world-planners, who claim that if America would quit feeding its grain to beef cattle, the whole world would have more bread. Those of this school of thought claim that America's love for grain-fed beef causes millions to starve to death by reducing the world's grain supply.[43]

Oftentimes abstentionists bring in 1 Corinthians 8:13 to supplement their exposition of Romans 14:21. The Corinthians verse reads, "Therefore, if food causes my brother to stumble, I will never eat meat again, that I might not cause my brother to stumble." Several observations will help put this class of verses on Christian liberty into a proper perspective:

First, quite obviously Paul puts the religiously scrupled abstainers in the category of the "weak": (a) He couples abstinence from meat and wine together. Earlier he taught that those who abstain from meat were not strong (Rom. 14:1). (b) The previous verses warn of the danger of the weak stumbling at the liberty of the strong. That is precisely what he is speaking of in verse 21. (c) He is persuaded that nothing is unclean of itself (vv. 14, 20) but that the uncleanness arises in the mind of the partaker (v. 23).

Second, Paul gives the admonition here in a specific social context; the strong must abstain on the occasions when it would possibly lure the weaker believers to stumble (i.e., actually sin against their consciences). When Paul says it is good not "to eat" and not "to drink" he does so by employing the aorist infinitive. Blass De Brunner's classic work, *A Greek Grammar of the New Testament*, comments on the aorist infinitive in this specific instance: "The aorist is to be taken strictly: 'it is good not to eat meat *for once* (in a specific instance) if it might cause offense'; it is not a question of continuous abstention."[44]

In his commentary, Lenski agrees: "The aorists are to be understood exactly: eating at one time ... in a given case, where offense would be caused; permanent abstinence is not discussed."[45] Jamieson, Fausset, and Brown note in their commentary that Paul's "directions are to be considered not as prescriptions for one's entire lifetime, even to promote the good of men on a large scale, but simply as cautions against the too free use of Christian liberty."[46] Clearly the prohibition against meat or wine is not a universally mandatory obligation. Scripture simply enjoins it upon strong believers when the real possibility exists that a brother may in fact be lured into doing that which he personally deems to be evil.

Third, we must understand 1 Corinthians 8:13 similarly. There Paul says he would "never eat meat again." Consider the following observations on this statement: (a) He does not say that he was, in fact, abstaining from meat because some stumble over the practice. He speaks in a conditional sense: "if." (b) Paul does not apostolically command others to this practice. It is Paul's personal testimony as to how he would choose to handle a specific situation. This is similar to his testimony in 1 Corinthians 7:7-8, where Paul suggests that it is good for the unmarried to remain so, "even as I." Note the lack of an imperative exhortation and the personal reference to himself: "I will never eat meat again." (c) Paul conditions all of this on a certain circumstance: He will not eat meat ever again *if* his eating would cause a brother to *stumble* (i.e., sin against his conscience and be destroyed). Certainly we cannot think that everywhere Paul goes and in every moment of his life, fragile Christians crowd around him ready to stumble over this issue.

Fourth, in the broader context of Paul's teaching we find a two-fold reason for any temporary abstinence from food, wine, or any such thing: (a) He would abstain in order not to prompt a weaker brother into actually sinning against his conscience (see previous discussion). (b) He would abstain in order to assist the weaker brother in overcoming his unnecessary scrupulosity. In 1 Corinthians 9:20-23 we learn that he would adopt the position of the weaker brother in order to establish a point of contact with him — with the ultimate hope of winning him out of his weakness. That is, Paul has a goal to train the weaker brother in strength — not to confirm his ill-founded religious scrupulosity and establish him in his weakness.[47] "To the weak I became weak, *that* [*hina*, in order that] I might win the weak " (1 Cor. 9:22). The Christian does the weaker brother no favor by confirming him in his weakness. With a balanced and gentle approach and patient teaching, the weak can become strong.

> **Romans 14:22-23**: The faith which you have, have as your own conviction before God. Happy is he who does not condemn himself in what he approves. But he who doubts is condemned if he eats, because his eating is not from faith; and whatsoever is not from faith is sin.

Clearly, Paul does not request the strong to relinquish their convictions. In fact, he could *never* do so — those convictions are proper in terms of a biblical, godly worldview. Rather, he exhorts them to avoid brandishing Christian liberty unlovingly and unwisely. Bible-based convictions are good and should be used in a way pleasing before God. The strong one can happily eat meat and drink wine, because his conscience does not condemn him (and properly so) in approving what he eats and drinks.

If a man, however, doubts it is right to eat meat or drink wine, and yet persists in eating or drinking in defiance of what he thinks is the will of God, then he is condemning himself. We must always strive for a clear conscience before God (Acts 24:16; 1 Tim. 1:3-5) because "whatsoever is not of faith is sin."

SUMMARY OF PRINCIPLES

The foregoing study is necessary for setting up the proper biblical understanding of the oft-misunderstood doctrine of Christian liberty. Unfortunately, it is somewhat lengthy, encumbered with exegetical and theological detail, and laboriously footnoted. The following summation concisely distills the principles contained in Romans 14. The verse references cue the reader not only to the biblical text, but back to the preceding commentary on the text.

1. *The church is a mixed body.* Within the church exist Christians at all levels of growth and maturation. Some are weak in the faith (vv. 1, 2, 23; 15:1) — whether due to newness in the faith (1 Pet. 2:2) or to "spiritual retardation" (Heb. 5:12-14) or for whatever reason. Yet, others are strong in their faith (vv. 2, 13, 22; 15:1). This polarity undoubtedly exists not only in the Roman situation, but in every church throughout the course of church history.

2. *Christians have love obligations toward each other.* The strong must fully accept the weak into their Christian fellowship and community (vv. 1, 3, 10; 15:1). Christianity is not elitist. We are all members of the body of Christ through his sovereign action in overcoming our sinful rebellion, not by our own purity, wisdom, or effort. Yet the weak are also

under apostolic obligation not to criticize the strong for their God-approved convictions (vv. 3, 4, 10).

3. *The ultimate authority over the Christian is the Lord.* The Lord, and he alone, is the only Lord over an individual's conscience (vv. 3, 4, 7-9, 12-13, 22). To him we stand or fall; to him must we give a final account. And the Lord does not abandon us to grope in darkness regarding his will for us; he has given us his word to lead us in the paths of righteousness (2 Tim. 3:16-17; Ps. 119:105). We must live by every word that proceeds out of God's mouth, not man's (Deut. 8:4).

4. *We must live according to our convictions.* As long as we hold something as a devout conviction before God, we must consistently live out that conviction (vv. 5, 12, 22-23). The essence of sin is living against God (Gen. 3:1-5; 1 John 3:4). Consequently, if we truly and deeply believe some conviction derives from God's will, we must live in terms of that belief until we abandon it on the basis of further evidence from Scripture. Peter finally abandons ceremonial food laws (which were legally disestablished at the cross, Eph. 2:15) under the influence of divine revelation through a vision (Acts 10:9-17).

5. *Christians must not be judgmental toward one another.* If an express command or a clear principle drawn by good and necessary inference from Scripture does not prohibit an action, then we cannot judge those who engage in such conduct (vv. 10, 13, 19). Otherwise we are condemning what God approves, making ourselves holier than God (Matt. 15:1-14).

6. *We must live responsibly toward one another.* The strong believer must not abuse his Christian liberty by enticing, prompting, or ensnaring weaker Christians into sinning against their own deeply rooted convictions. That is, the stronger believer must be careful not to put the weaker

believer in a position wherein he will actually breach his own convictions (vv. 13, 15, 16, 20-23). This is to tempt the weaker brother into an "attitudinal sin." That is, even though the action itself is not sinful, the fact that the weaker brother *believes* it to be sinful makes it a sin for him. He would then be engaging in a course of action that was for him direct rebellion against God.

7. *Nothing in God's creation is intrinsically evil.* Evil is a moral condition operative in free moral agents, whether angelic or human. Sin is not a material property somehow rooted in tangible creation (vv. 14, 20). As the Lord himself teaches:

> Listen to Me, all of you, and understand: there is nothing outside the man which going into him can defile him; but the things which proceed out of the man are what defile the man.... For from within, out of the heart of men, proceed the evil thoughts, fornications, thefts, murders, adulteries, deeds of coveting and wickedness, as well as deceit, sensuality, envy, slander, pride and foolishness. All these evil things proceed from within and defile the man. (Mark 7:14-15, 21-23)

8. *Love and peace must characterize Christian relations* (vv. 15, 17, 19). We are all brothers in Christ, members of one body (1 Cor. 12:12-27). We must therefore work together as a body to the glory of God (Eph. 4:1-6). Indeed, the Lord Jesus Christ posits this as a mark of discipleship: "By this all men will know that you are My disciples, if you have love for one another" (John 13:35).

9. *We must on occasion deny ourselves for the good of our brothers.* Certain occasions may arise wherein it may be best to temporarily and voluntarily abstain from certain actions (e.g., partaking of wine, eating meat, and so forth) that are otherwise good. This duty befalls us if such actions pose a

real danger to luring a weaker Christian to act contrarily to the dictates of his moral and spiritual conscience (v. 21; 1 Cor. 8:13).

10. *We must all seek to grow in grace.* The strong should rejoice in their knowledge of God's approval (vv. 18, 22) and should gently and patiently seek to win the weak to a stronger position (15:1; 1 Cor. 9:20-23). Unfortunately, oftentimes Christians expect the strong to come around to the weaker brother's position, thereby confirming the weak in his weakness.

CONCLUSION

Christians must be careful not only to encourage the strong to patiently forgo his privilege on just occasion, but must also exhort the weak to refrain from judging the stronger. The issue of Christian liberty involves *mutual* concern and edification. Christian liberty is a two-way street paved with love. We must not prefer one class of believers above the other.

As I conclude the present study on Christian liberty, the following paragraphs by Charles Hodge and John Calvin merit close attention. Beginning with Hodge:

> The gospel does not make religion to consist in external observances.... It is a great error in morals, and a great practical evil, to make that sinful which is in fact innocent. Christian love never requires this or any other sacrifice of truth. Paul would not consent, for the sake of avoiding offence, that eating all kinds of food, even what had been offered to idols, or disregarding sacred festivals of human appointment, should be made a sin; he strenuously and openly maintained the reverse. He represents those who thought differently, as weak in faith, as being under an error, from which more knowledge and more piety would free them....

We should stand fast in the liberty wherewith Christ has made us free, and not allow our consciences to be brought under the yoke of bondage to human opinions. There is a strong tendency in men to treat, as matters of conscience, things which God has never enjoined....

It is often necessary to assert our Christian liberty at the expense of incurring censure, and offending even good men, in order that right principles of duty may be preserved. Our Saviour consented to be regarded as a Sabbath-breaker, and even a "wine bibber and a friend of publicans and sinners"; but wisdom was justified of her children.[48]

Elsewhere Hodge provides us with the following insights into the matter:

It is morally obligatory, therefore, to abstain from indulging in things indifferent, when the use of them is the occasion of sin to others. This is a principle the application of which must be left to every man's conscience in the fear of God. No rule of conduct, founded on expediency, can be enforced by church discipline. It was right in Paul to refuse to eat flesh for fear of causing others to offend; but he could not have been justly exposed to discipline, had he seen fit to eat it. He circumcised Timothy, and refused to circumcise Titus. Whenever a thing is right or wrong according to circumstances, every man must have the right to judge of those circumstances.[49]

In his *Institutes of the Christian Religion*, Calvin helps us to make a vital distinction in Christian liberty when he speaks of the difference between an "offense given" and an "offense received" (or taken):

Here, then, I shall say something about offenses — how they are to be distinguished, which ones avoided, which overlooked. From this we may afterward be able to determine what place there is for our freedom among men. Now I like that common distinction between an offense given and one received, inasmuch as it has the clear support of Scripture and properly expresses what is meant.

If you do anything with unseemly levity, or wantonness, or rashness, out of its proper order or place, so as to cause the ignorant and the simple to stumble, such will be called an offense given by you, since by your fault it came about that this sort of offense arose. And, to be sure, one speaks of an offense as given in some matter when its fault arises from the doer of the thing itself.

An offense is spoken of as received when something, otherwise not wickedly or unseasonably committed, is by ill will or malicious intent of mind wrenched into occasion for offense. Here is no "given" offense.[50]

CHAPTER 7

COMMON OBJECTIONS CONSIDERED

$\mathbf{M}$y main objective in this book is to analyze what the Bible says about wine drinking, and that has been my unrelenting focus. Nevertheless, various objections arise to the moderationist position to which I should respond, even if only briefly. My responses will demonstrate the application of the biblical principles to common objections or concerns. I will respond to the main questions that arise in our debate: What about the potential alcoholic? How much is too much? Health and alcohol? Christian witness? What does the Bible say about diluted wine?

THE "POTENTIAL ALCOHOLIC"

Christian abstentionists and prohibitionists often express the fear that the moderationist position has dangerous implications for the "potential alcoholic." Generally this question presupposes a genetic predisposition to alcoholism. Certainly different people have various levels of tolerance to alcohol. But the notion that alcoholism is somehow a physiological defect is antithetical to the biblical doctrine of sin and of personal responsibility.[1]

The Bible clearly condemns drunkenness as a moral failure and a spiritual sin, showing that it is a matter of personal responsibility (Gal. 5:19-21). In fact, chronic drunkenness effectively bars entrance into the kingdom of God, showing that men must turn from it (1 Cor. 6:9-10). Consequently, what becomes of God's justice if he bars from his kingdom "physiological defectives" whom he has made (Ex. 4:11)? Surely the Lord would not punish someone for a genetic fault or a physiological malformity.

Furthermore, other problems arise when we assert that imbibing alcohol is a form of reckless social conduct in light of the many unknown "potential alcoholics." Such a position impugns the character of both the apostles and even the Lord Jesus Christ himself. Did they not partake of wine openly (Luke 7:33-35)? Were they guilty of endangering those who were "physiologically defective"? Did they leave a bad example for future Christians? Was Jesus ignorant of "potential alcoholics" or of "constitutional alcoholism"?

Along these lines, comments by Christian ethicist and philosopher Greg L. Bahnsen may prove helpful. He is dealing with an analogous ethical situation, although not identical to alcohol use. In this case he answers arguments that homosexuality is a problem of physiological constitution or genetic predisposition:

> In a theological context it might mean that the depraved nature with which men are born is for some individuals specifically oriented to the sinful perversion of homosexuality. However, the Scripture does not support the idea that each person receives a sinful nature with a peculiar bent toward particular transgressions of God's will. Every man inherits a general depravity of heart, a fundamental disinclination to good, a pervasive misdirection, which affects every aspect of his person without discriminating emphases; there is a wholesale, general pollution operating in everything he is and does. Nevertheless, the ways in which individual sinners develop their depraved natures, the particular sins upon which they focus and around which their characters are formed, will differ from person to person.[2]

Bahnsen's comments clearly and easily apply to the matter we are considering.

Alcoholism researcher John Langone writes:

> Heredity, errors in the body's chemistry that prevent the alcoholic from using alcohol properly, brain defects, allergy, vitamin deficiency, glandular problems, a defective "thermostat" that causes an uncontrollable thirst for alcohol all have been examined by researchers. But thus far, none has been shown to be specifically responsible for alcoholism. There is no physical examination or blood test that can yet be performed to determine why a person has become an alcoholic, or whether he or she will become one; and no one has isolated a specific gene, that unit of heredity, for alcoholism.[3]

This is not to trivialize the truly serious problem of alcohol abuse. Many people have serious problems with alcohol — but the problem is due to moral failure, not physiological defect. Circumspect Christians should be aware of the sinful tendencies of acquaintances and should avoid causing them to "stumble" by tempting them to partake.

HOW MUCH IS TOO MUCH?

A charge related to the previous is the problem of *defining* the immoderate consumption of alcohol. Wilkerson asks, "But what is moderation?" and, "Who is the referee in this moderation game Christians play?"[4] Reynolds ponders this "problem" as well: "If some alcohol for pleasure or relief from tension or for sociability is permitted and 'much' prohibited, the question must arise, how much is 'much'?"[5] Elsewhere he asks, "How can we be sure when the amount of any toxic substance we may take into our bodies may become sinful in his holy eyes?"[6]

Obviously the Christian must avoid drunkenness

resulting from overindulgence. And just as obviously different people have different capacities or tolerances for safe and wholesome alcohol consumption. But to ask these questions is not to answer them. That is, posing the questions in the present debate does not disallow all alcohol consumption, for there *is* in fact a difference between light drinking and heavy drinking. Note that:

First, the Bible *does* in fact command us to avoid "much" drink. If it were impossible to draw a morally relevant distinction between "much" drinking and moderate drinking, why does God bother to warn us against "much" drinking? The moral problem of alcohol consumption is not defining *quantity* of alcohol consumed (in ounces), but its *effect* (in moral impact). The danger level will certainly differ from person to person; nevertheless, a difference exists between someone drunk and someone *not* drunk. After all, how could Scripture condemn "drunkenness" if we cannot tell the difference?

Second, we cannot limit the definitional problem of "drunkenness" simply to the consumption of alcohol alone. We may demonstrate the *reductio ad absurdum* in the argument by noting that Scripture also condemns "gluttony" (Deut. 21:20; Prov. 23:20-21; 28:7; Matt. 11:19; Luke 7:34; Titus 1:12). Scientifically speaking, who can define "gluttony"? Who can say with any authority how much food is *too* much food to ingest? Yet, as a matter of biblical fact, gluttony is a sin.

Third, interestingly, even *water* can cause drunkenness — when too much is consumed. Medical scientists have documented cases of "water intoxication." Obviously Scripture does not prohibit us from drinking water because we cannot *in advance* define the quantity that leads to "water intoxication."[7]

ALCOHOL AND HEALTH

Christian theology recognizes two important truths regarding man's body: (1) Creationally, the body of man is a glorious creation of God (Gen. 2:7; Ps. 139:13-16) and (2) redemptively, the Christian's body is the "temple of the Holy Spirit" (1 Cor. 6:19). These twin truths of creation and redemption exercise a direct and important bearing on the Christian's concern for health.[8]

Prohibitionists often allege that alcohol consumption per se is hazardous to one's health. As I state in the introduction to this book, my design is not to explore the medical implications of alcohol use. I will touch very briefly upon it here, though. Of course, I am not a medical doctor (having a Th.D. means I can remove an appendix from a book, but not from a person) and I am not offering medical advice. I have collected the medical material below from peer-reviewed, published scientific reports; it is not designed to dispense medical advice nor promote drinking for health purposes. Nevertheless, in response to concerns over health matters, I should note two important points.

The first is that Scripture implies that alcoholic beverages are not detrimental to good health in a normal, healthy person. Were they hazardous both the integrity of Scripture and the goodness of God would be called into question. In Chapters 2 through 5, I amply demonstrate from Scripture that God allows alcoholic beverages for Christian use. Indeed, alcoholic wine is a worthy gift between righteous men and is even deemed a blessing from God. Furthermore, I note that Christ himself partook of wine and that he even established the Lord's Supper with it. Surely all of this is not detrimental to man's health considerations. As a matter of fact, Paul even exhorts Timothy to take a little wine for reasons of *better* health (1 Tim. 5:23).

The second is that except for those with a vehement predisposition against alcoholic beverages, a growing volume of medical research over the past twenty years suggests that moderate alcohol consumption is actually *beneficial* to one's health. I will allow quite a bit more space on this second point because I have not dealt with it in the previous chapters.

Morris Chafetz, M.D., has an enlightening observation:

> Between effects of heavy or excessive alcohol intake and moderate drinking there is a great distinction. Excessive consumption increases mortality and produces various types of damage.... However, there is no evidence of damaging effects even from the steady intake of moderate amounts and, indeed, mortality statistics ... suggest a possible beneficial effect.[9]

This positive effect of alcohol on the human body seems especially related to the heart. As the National Institute on Alcohol and Alcohol Abuse notes, "Some epidemiological data suggest that the risk for coronary artery disease may be smaller in light drinkers than abstainers."[10] A more recent report by this alcohol abuse agency confirms this research.[11]

The American Heart Association reports that "analyses showed that compared with non-drinkers, people who drank 'moderate' amounts of alcohol every day — defined as two beers or wines or one mixed drink — had a 49 percent lower risk of a heart attack."[12]

Numerous studies confirm such evidence. An important medical report published in the mid-1980s noted that "the results indicated that moderate consumers (1 to 2 drinks/day) were at a lower risk of coronary heart disease than the non consumers or heavy consumers. Evolution of total mortality in relationship to alcohol consumption reveals that a similar u-shaped relationship to longevity exists."[13] This report continues: "Increased consumption over time preceded the decline in cardiovascular disease mortality on a population basis."[14]

Thomas Turner, president of the Johns Hopkins Alcoholic Beverage Medical Research Foundation reported in 1985, "It is very interesting and the results look quite clear. There is a great deal of evidence accumulating all over the Western world that moderate drinking is associated with better health.... Moderate drinking does not have any chronic effects. That's one message that comes through quite clear."[15]

News on alcohol's positive effect on the heart erupted on the social scene with a *60 Minutes* television report on November 17, 1991. The report, which caused quite a stir, noted the surprising "French Paradox," which observes that despite a diet that scientists warn is harmful to health, the French people have a statistically low number of heart problems. This phenomenon is considered a direct result of their consuming statistically higher rates of alcohol.

A 1996 *Newsweek* report noted that the United States Department of Health and Human Services "came up with the first pro-alcohol message in the history of federal health policy."[16] In fact, "the good news keeps on coming: moderate drinkers live longer, moderate drinkers get fewer colds, moderate drinkers have flatter stomachs, moderate drinkers who happen to eat bad oysters don't get as sick."[17] It even reported that "compared with real wine-drinking countries, the United States is practically dry. That may be a reason, scientists say, that our rate of heart disease is higher."[18]

A 1997 Associated Press release quotes Dr. Vincent Figueredo, a San Francisco General Hospital cardiologist and author of a University of California, San Francisco, health study: "Moderate consumption after a heart attack cut cell death in half and almost doubled the recovery of muscle function in the heart."[19]

In a 1999 news report we read of medical research regarding strokes: "The new data supports the guidelines of the National Stroke Association, which say moderate drinkers might protect themselves from strokes by continuing to consume alcohol."[20] In fact, the report noted that "drinking up to two alcoholic drinks per day reduced the risk of stroke by half."[21]

In response to such overwhelming evidence, Stephen Reynolds expresses grave doubts. Of the moderationist arguments in this regard, he wonders: "The medical authorities they seem to prefer may be subsidized by the liquor industry." He even writes regarding Paul's advice to Timothy in 1 Timothy 5:23 (which relates only to the stomach): "But for Timothy's stomach he could never have recommended alcohol. It is known now, and was probably known then, that alcohol does nothing good to the stomach." He then insists that Paul's prescription called for pure, unfermented grape juice.†

† Reynolds, *Alcohol,* 33, 55. Remember: Reynolds argues that references to "wine" in a good sense in the Bible cannot refer to alcoholic wine. In light of this principle of interpretation, one must wonder why the Good Samaritan poured grape juice in the wounds of the assaulted Jew in Luke 10:34!

Contrary to both the general tendency of Reynolds' position with regard to alcohol and health and his specific comments on 1 Timothy 5:23, Raymond McCarthy, the editor of *Drinking and Intoxication,* writes:

> In moderate amounts alcohol stimulates the flow of gastric juices and promotes stomach motility.... There is no evidence that alcohol ever causes gastric ulcers; doctors forbid their ulcer patients to drink because of the increased gastric flow. Moderate amounts of alcohol do not interfere with digestion; they may even promote it.[22]

Many prohibitionists warn that alcohol itself is a poison and should be avoided by Christians for reasons of good health. Reynolds insists that the alcohol of fermented wine is a poison. In his most recent book on the subject we read of his study of Hosea 7:5: "The concern of this study is to prove that the Bible says that alcoholic wine is a poison."[†] "It is the poison *of* wine, that is the poison of alcohol, the poison in grape juice which has fermented."[23] And later still he vigorously opposes alcohol in that it is a "poisonous drug" and could not be used as "a type of the Lord's Supper."[24] Thus, his argument quite vigorously asserts the danger of drinking "poison" when we drink wine. But is his argument legitimate?

† Reynolds, *Biblical*, 63. If "alcoholic wine" is a poison, why does not Scripture have a special term for it?

In the first place, we should note that "alcohol is normally present in all mammals" in their intestines.[25]

Gene Ford notes:

> Not only is alcohol abundant in nature, but it is produced and eliminated regularly and naturally within every human body. Alcohol is a natural bodily fluid.
>
> Ethyl alcohol is not foreign to human physiology. Up to one ounce is produced daily in humans by bacterial breakdown of starches and sugars. Small amounts of alcohol are consumed in fruit juices and medicines.[26]

Clearly then, alcohol is a *naturally occurring* product of mammalian physiology — as created by God. In fact, Reynolds himself admits this: "Modern science has determined that alcohol is normally present in mammals, being produced in the intestinal tract."[27]

In the second place, Reynolds' understanding of alcohol as poison is not in accord with medical authorities. For instance, the *Illustrated Encyclopedia of Family Health* notes,

"Even water and oxygen, when present in excess, can cause damage to the body.... So a poison must be defined as any substance that is given in sufficient quantity to damage the normal working of the body" (italics mine for emphasis).[28] Under the heading "Poisons and Poisoning" in the *Encyclopedia Britannica, Macropaedia* (15th ed., vol. 25, p. 895), we read, "Poisons are substances that in small amounts are capable of producing serious injury or death. In truth, however, the poison is in the dose." Can alcohol in "small amounts" produce "serious injury or death" to a normal, healthy person? As evidenced by the medical data just quoted, I think it's safe to answer that as "No."

† Confusion reigns among the general populace about the effects of drinking on fetal development; moderate drinking apparently has no deleterious effect on the child. Regarding fetal alcohol syndrome (FAS), "The typical profile of the FAS mother is a 30-plus-year old alcoholic in poor health, taking poor nutrition, smoking, living in an alcoholic environmental home or in the company of a male alcoholic.... FAS children are generally exposed to ponderously abusive amounts of alcoholic wine not likely to be confused by 'moderate' here.... There have been no known cases of 'full blown' FAS in children whose mothers consumed moderate amounts of alcohol." See: Shoemaker, 13.

Of course, none of this — whether from the Bible or scientific data — denies the obvious fact that certain physiological abnormalities (e.g., allergies, liver malfunction) and particular conditions (e.g., pregnancy)† may preclude the safe consumption of alcohol. This is true not only of alcohol but other substances, such as cow's milk, caffeine, penicillin, aspirin, and any number of other things. Nevertheless, we cannot credibly argue in general that alcoholic beverages are harmful to health.

ALCOHOL AND THE CHRISTIAN WITNESS

Abstainers often argue that Christians should totally abstain from alcohol as a witness to both our sinful, hedonistic culture and to our own weaker Christian brothers. For instance, Harold Lindsell writes:

> When one considers these statistics [i.e., demographic studies on alcohol abuse] and ponders the numerous drawbacks to the use of alcohol, it remains for those who advocate its use to demonstrate its value and benefits. There is no argument in its favor that is not outweighed by the drawbacks. The Christian has a particular responsibility in this matter because of the significance his lifestyle and influence have on others.[29]

Gleason Archer, conservative Old Testament scholar, agrees. "If we really care about the souls of men, and if we are really in business for Christ rather than for ourselves," he writes, "then there seems (to this writer, at least) to be no alternative to total abstinence not as a matter of legalism, but rather as a matter of love."[30] Even moderationist Andre Bustanoby confesses, "I like the idea of pastors being total abstainers for the sake of example."[31]

Certainly Christians must be examples to others (1 Tim. 4:12; 1 Cor. 4:16; 11:1). This witness-by-example is an important aspect of our calling to glorify God in all of life (Phil. 2:15; Titus 2:8; 1 Pet. 2:11-12). For several reasons, however, it does not follow that a moderate partaking of alcoholic beverages is contrary to a full-orbed Christian witness.

First, in Scripture the Lord and his apostles partake of wine. And they do so despite sinful men indulging in it to their own hurt and degradation. The Bible frequently and unsparingly condemns drunkenness, which shows that "the Bible affords ample proof that excessive drinking of intoxicants was a common vice among the Hebrews, as among other ancient peoples."[32]

Second, biblical truth must mold the character of the Christian witness. The truth is that the Bible does not condemn moderate consumption of alcohol. The "Christian witness" argument cannot schizophrenically maintain that Christians are obligated to avoid that which Scripture allows! We detract from, not enhance, our witness if we promote a false morality, a morality presumably "higher" than the Bible, a morality in *contradiction* to Scripture. The biblical witness regarding alcohol should be that of moderation (Acts 24:25; Gal. 5:23).

Third, temporary abstinence should witness against the sinner's weakness, not against God's creation. Even in those cases where temporarily abstaining is prudent as a matter of witness, the goal of such must be to expose the sinfulness of the sinner's weakness. When Paul becomes "all things to all men" (e.g., when he abstains from wine in the presence of the weak), he does so with the long-range goal of demonstrating the failure of weakness and the error of the abstentionist and prohibitionist position. In 1 Corinthians 9:22 he writes, "To the weak I became weak." This is not to encourage them in their weakness; nor is it Paul's adoption of a permanent lifestyle. He continues, "To the weak I became weak, *that I might win the weak*." Paul's temporary abstinence, for example, would be ultimately to show the weak his error and to win him away from his weakness, his misapprehension of biblical morality. This is not to say that the moderationist seeks to get the "weaker" brother to drink. Rather that we encourage the weaker brother to see the error of his position, not necessarily to change his practice and begin drinking.

Fourth, principles of abstinence can go too far. Such a principle of conduct knows no limits and can lead to all manner of erroneous prohibitions, thereby becoming neo-Pharasaism. In earlier comments I note that some deem America's love for beef to be sinful in light of world hunger.

Allegedly our grain-fed beef consumes an "unfair" amount of the world's grain supply. As a matter of Christian witness, some might encourage abstaining from beef as a Christian witness. We could multiply such radical (but internally logical) calls for abstinence in illustrating the failure of the "Christian witness" argument. If we draw our moral guidelines from Scripture, however, we do not allow free rein to the imagination or cultural holiness.

THINNING WINE WITH WATER

Some who deem wine drinking as everywhere and always evil will concede that fermented wine was actually drunk in the Bible. But they will then insist that it was always diluted with water.† For a variety of reasons, this objection does not undercut the moderationist position.

First, *all* the evidence supporting this contention comes from extra-biblical sources such as Pliny's *Natural History*.[33] Note, however, that Scripture references to "mixed wine," such as Chapters 9 and 23 of Proverbs and Isaiah 65, are not about wine mixed with water. These texts do not mention "water" in the mix. In fact, Psalm 65:8 would be inexplicable if we assume such a mix:

† In fact, we often hear arguments that weakened, watered wine was preferred in antiquity. But if that were true, we must wonder at how much abuse of wine arose from such! Pliny writes that wine "caused the commission of thousands of crimes" (*Nat. Hist.* 14:28). Obviously *even on this assumption* we still have to deal with widespread drunkenness.

> For a cup is in the hand of the LORD, and the wine foams;
> It is well mixed, and He pours out of this;
> Surely all the wicked of the earth must drain and drink down
> its dregs.

Is this symbol of God's wine really wine "well mixed" with water?

In the Old Testament the ancients sometimes mixed wine with spices for flavor enhancement. In the Song of Solomon, the bride sings to her beloved:

> I would lead you and bring you
> Into the house of my mother, who used to instruct me;
> I would give you spiced wine to drink from the juice of my pomegranates. (8:2)

In fact, the Brown, Driver, and Briggs lexicon notes that the root word for "mixed" means to "make a choice drink by mixing with spices, etc." And, to further make the case, they specifically comment that "mixing with water came later, cf. 2 Macc 15:39."[34]

Second, nowhere does the biblical record distinguish "undiluted" (so-called unsafe) wine from "water diluted" (so-called safe) wine. Were it actually a mark of righteousness to avoid undiluted wine and to enjoy only diluted wine, why then is the Scripture silent on the matter? After all, is not the Scripture "profitable for teaching, for reproof, for correction, for training in righteousness; that the man of God may be adequate, equipped for every good work" (2 Tim. 3:16-17)?

Third, recognized biblical scholars of every stripe are in virtual agreement on the nondiluted nature of wine in the Old Testament. Emmet Russell is apparently of the abstentionist persuasion in that he writes, "Whatever use Jesus or others made of wine is no proof that its use in our tense age is wise. The Bible gives more space to the danger than to the benefit of wine."[35] Yet in the same context he also categorically states that "in OT times wine was not diluted." Burton Scott Easton agrees: "In OT times wine was drunk undiluted, and wine mixed with water was thought to be ruined."[36]

Fourth, although numerous passages speak of "mixed wines" (some referring to different wines mixed together, others to wines mixed with various herbs and spices), only one passage mentions water-diluted wine. Isaiah 1:22 laments, "Your silver has become dross, your drink diluted with water."[37]

Interestingly, this sole reference to water-diluted wine speaks of such a practice in a *negative* manner. Old Testament scholar E. J. Young comments on the "dilution" or "weakening" of wine in this passage:

> weakened — Literally, "cut." By means of cutting, the strength of wine is impaired. *Sov'ek* is fine wine, used here in parallelism with *kaspeck*, "thy silver." The metal that was so pure that light could find in it a clear reflection, as well as the fine wine of the land, was destroyed, the wine having been weakened (lit., cut, mutilated, circumcised, castrated) by water.[38]

The statement here seems to be based partly in actual fact and partly in figurative allusion. That is, the city of Jerusalem, which has become a "harlot" filled with "murderers" (Is. 1:21), is guilty also of both monetary inflation (a means of governmental theft) and product debasement (a means of commercial theft). By adding a measure of dross to the silver, a given weight of the precious metal could be fraudulently increased. By cutting fine wine with water, the total volume output of wine could be increased, while the actual quality of each unit sold would be diminished.

Undoubtedly, this reference alludes to crimes actually being committed. But they also serve as figurative symbols for the debasement of the moral and spiritual character of Israel in that day. Ironically, then, the *only* biblical reference to water-diluted wine appears in a context of rebuke!

Interestingly, graffiti from Pompeii shows that the ancients prefer undiluted wine: "Curses on you, landlord, you sell water and drink unmixed wine yourself."[39]

CONCLUSION

I am firmly convinced that the positive, exegetically derived, theologically coherent evidence that I present in Chapters 2 through 6 clearly allow Christians the right to partake of alcoholic beverages in moderation. These final objections addressed in this chapter fail of their purpose in overthrowing the strong case for moderate consumption of alcohol. We may learn additional helpful information from these concerns, but our case for moderation is not thereby undercut, but rather strengthened.

CHAPTER 8
CONCLUSION

The thrust of my study is intentionally narrow. My concern is to research and analyze the *biblical* data regarding the general question of the morality of alcohol consumption. Though other issues might tangentially bear upon the topic, the ultimate issue is: What saith the Lord?

In the final analysis it seems abundantly clear that Scripture neither urges universal total abstinence nor demands absolute prohibition. Although alcoholic beverages can be, have been, and are presently abused by individuals, such need not be the case. Indeed, the biblical record frequently and clearly speaks of alcoholic beverages as good gifts from God for man's enjoyment. Unfortunately, as is always the case among sinners, good things are often transformed into curses. This is true not only with alcohol but with food, medicine, sex, wealth, authority, and many other areas of life.

The reader should not conclude that I intend for this study to encourage drinking by those who do not presently do so. I do not. I have never and will never encourage others to drink. In fact, I seldom drank wine even before discovering my own liver problem. At the most I only drank five or six glasses of wine *a year*. Whether or not an individual wants to drink is a matter of his own tastes and discretion, within biblical limits, of course.

Neither should you think that this study presents all that can be said on the whole question of alcohol. For instance, there are various state concerns and obligations that undoubtedly justify some government involvement in the use of alcohol — perhaps forbidding consumption for certain ages and under certain conditions, punishing abuse of alcoholic beverages, ensuring reasonable health standards relative to its production, enforcing truth-in-advertising in its promotion, and so forth. These and numerous other aspects of the alcohol question deserve consideration.

The only concern I place before the reader is the question of whether or not God allows alcohol consumption. Too often the Bible takes the back seat in social and cultural arguments for and against alcohol. This is most unfortunate — especially when considering the matter in Christian circles. If believers are to reconstruct society in terms of their cultural mandate and along the lines of biblical law, they must do so out of intense reflection on what the Bible actually says. They must, as Paul tells us in the third chapter of Romans, "let God be found true."

And the LORD of hosts will prepare
a lavish banquet for all peoples...
A banquet of aged wine,
choice pieces with marrow,
And refined aged wine.
Isaiah 25:6

The Son of Man has come eating and drinking...
wisdom is vindicated by all her children.
Luke 7:33-35

CHAPTER CITATIONS

CHAPTER 1

[1] For a brief history see: Fleming, Chs 6-7.

[2] Noll, 32.

[3] Wilkerson, 65.

[4] Wilkerson, 12.

[5] Van Impe, 149.

[6] Reynolds, *Biblical*, 107.

[7] Reynolds, *Biblical*, 68.

[8] Teachout, 330.

[9] Reynolds, *Biblical*, 183.

[10] Van Impe, 8.

[11] Reynolds, *Biblical*, 147.

[12] Wilkerson, 35.

[13] Reynolds, *Biblical*, 66.

[14] Reynolds, *Biblical*, 68.

[15] Archer, 149.

[16] Gilchrist, 19-33.

[17] *Presbyterian Guardian*, 3.

[18] Lindsell, 116.

[19] Dunn, 11.

[20] Gentry and Reynolds, 41-49.

[21] Williams, 27.

[22] Cited by Schnucker, 756.

[23] Kuiper, 17.

CHAPTER 2

[1] Gentry, *Greatness*; North, *Dominion Covenant*.

[2] Lee, *Central Significance*.

[3] Cited in Kobler, 33.

[4] Chafetz, 65.

[5] For instance, the vomiting associated with excessive consumption can lead to esophagitis due to the increased acid production by the stomach and frequent agitation of the esophagal lining by vomiting action. For additional medical research on the effects of chronic alcoholism see: O'Brien and Chafetz, *The Encyclopedia of Alcoholism* and *The Merck Manual of Diagnosis and Therapy*.

[6] Rushdoony, 293-301.

[7] Reynolds, *Biblical*, 128.

[8] Van Impe, 137.

CHAPTER 3

[1] Brown, Driver and Briggs, 406. See also: Harris, Archer and Waltke, 1:375.

[2] Brown, Driver and Briggs, 406; Harris, Archer and Waltke, 1:375. See also: Easton, 4:3086; Moore, 3:2536; Davis, 867.

[3] Brown, Driver and Briggs, 406.

[4] Harris, Archer and Waltke, 1:376.

[5] Strong, Hebrew dictionary entry #3196.

[6] Davidson, 303.

[7] Reynolds, *Biblical*, 33.

[8] Wilkerson, 19.

[9] From the foreword to Van Impe, 8.

[10] Reynolds, *Biblical*, 142.

[11] Fitzsimmonds, 1254.

[12] Davis, 867.

[13] Reynolds, *Biblical*, 70.

[14] Reynolds, *Biblical*, 69.

[15] Unger, 1168.

[16] Harris, 11.

[17] Harris, 7.

[18] Young, 3:193. See also: Alexander, 1:415; Barabas, 3:906.

[19] Tregelles, 838.

[20] Reynolds, *Biblical,*120; Patton, 21-45; Wilkerson, 26-30; Teachout, Appendix G.

[21] Reynolds, *Alcohol*, 20. Others promoting the same approach to Isaiah 16:10 include: Teachout, 282; Patton, 107; Ewing, 14.

[22] Reynolds, *Biblical*, 145.

[23] Kerr, 2:881.

[24] Unger, 1168.

[25] Reynolds, *Biblical*, 155.

[26] Moore, 3:2536-2537.

[27] Quoted in Reynolds, *Biblical*, 191.

[28] Reynolds, *Biblical*, 43.

[29] See pages 29, 43, 44, 56, 150.

[30] "Moses Stuart," 621. Cited in Reynolds, *Biblical*, 44.

[31] Patton, 55, 232.

[32] Teachout, 312.

[33] Van Impe, 175-180.

[34] Reynolds, *Biblical*, 24.

[35] Reynolds, *Alcohol*, 21.

[36] Reynolds, *Alcohol*, 21, 36.

[37] Reynolds, *Alcohol*, 36-37.

[38] Reynolds, *Alcohol*, 46.

[39] Reynolds, *Biblical*, 3.

[40] Reynolds, *Biblical*, 131. See other such references on pages 24, 25, 77, 93, 94.

[41] He cites Prov. 23:31 over twenty times in *Biblical Approach to Alcohol.*

[42] Reynolds, *Biblical*, 7.

[43] Reynolds, *Biblical*, 9. See his extensive argument on pages 7-11.

[44] Reynolds, *Biblical*, 77.

[45] Reynolds, *Biblical*, 74.

[46] Reynolds, *Biblical*, 78.

[47] Reynolds, *Biblical*, 157.

[48] Reynolds, *Biblical*, 24.

[49] Edersheim, *Temple*, 376.

[50] See discussions of this issue in: Hughes, 237ff; Pink, 360ff; Schultz, 2:1462ff; Spurgeon, 5:202.

[51] Harris, 14.

[52] Reynolds, *Biblical*, 80.

[53] Reynolds, *Biblical*, 80.

[54] Reynolds, *Biblical*, 68.

[55] Brown, Driver and Briggs, 440.

[56] Van Impe, 111.

[57] Gen. 27:28; 27:37; Deut. 7:13; Deut. 11:14; 12:17; 14:23; 18:4; 28:51; 33:28; 2 Chr. 31:5; Neh. 5:11; 10:39; Ps. 4:7; Is. 36:17; 62:8; Jer. 31:12; Hos. 2:8-9; 2:22; 7:14; Joel 1:10; 2:19; 2:24; Hag. 1:11; Zech. 9:17.

[58] Easton, 5:3086.

[59] Brown, Driver and Briggs; *tirosh* entry at 1066 refers to *yarash* entry at 440. The *yarash* entry on 439 yields this definition of the root verb itself.

[60] Reynolds, *Biblical*, 32.

[61] Reynolds, *Biblical*, 195.

[62] Fitzsimmonds, 1254.

[63] Brown, Driver and Briggs, 1016.

[64] Brown, Driver and Briggs, 1016.

[65] Gen. 9:20-27; 1 Sam. 25:36; 2 Sam. 13:28-29; 1 Kin. 16:9; 20:16; Jer. 13:13; Is. 63:6; 49:26; Harris, Archer and Waltke, 2:926.

[66] 1 Sam. 1:13; 25:36; 1 Kin. 16:9; 20:16; Prov. 26:9; Is. 19:14; 24:20; Jer. 23:9; Ps. 107:27; Harris, Archer and Waltke, 2:927.

[67] See: Jer. 13:13; Ezek. 23:33; 39:19;

Harris, Archer and Waltke, 2:927.

[68] Easton, 4:3086.

[69] Harris, Archer and Waltke, 2:926.

[70] Harris, 11.

[71] Kerr, 2:879.

[72] Kerr, 2:880.

[73] Brown, Driver and Briggs, 779.

[74] Morris, 162.

[75] The report clearly states its abstentionist character: On page 33 the committee "reaffirms its advocacy of total abstinence from the beverage use of alcohol" (Gilchrist, 33; see also p. 23, 36).

CHAPTER 4

[1] Thayer, 442.

[2] Abbott-Smith, 314: "in LXX chiefly for *yayin*."

[3] Liddell and Scott, 976.

[4] Liddell and Scott, 976.

[5] Arndt and Gingrich, 564.

[6] Davis, 867.

[7] Thayer, 490.

[8] Arndt and Gingrich, 721. *Prosechontas* means "occupy oneself with, devote or apply oneself to." It is used again in 1 Timothy 4:13 of devoting oneself to ministerial duties.

[9] Reynolds, *Alcohol*, 53.

[10] Nicoll and Bernard, 3:362.

[11] Nicoll and Bernard, 3:363.

[12] Thayer, 118.

[13] Edersheim, *Life and Times*, Book 4, Chapter 12.

[14] Reynolds, *Alcohol*, 39.

[15] Hendriksen, 115.

[16] Reynolds, *Alcohol*, 37-38.

[17] Reynolds, *Biblical*, 96.

[18] Reynolds, *Alcohol*, 37-39.

[19] Hendriksen, 115.

[20] Ellicott, 6:394. See also: Clarke, 5:527; Trench, 1:117.

[21] Reynolds, *Alcohol*, 37.

[22] Reynolds, *Alcohol*, 38-39.

[23] Preisker, 4:546.

[24] Priesker, 4:546.

[25] Priesker, 4:547.

[26] Parkhurst, 422.

[27] Reynolds, *Biblical*, 101.

[28] Seeseman, 5:163.

[29] Cited in Bustanoby, 41.

[30] Reynolds, *Biblical*, 108.

[31] Moore, 3:2537-2538.

[32] Davis, 868.

[33] Seeseman, 5:164.

[34] Buschel, 1:685; Behm, 3:733ff.; Dalman, 137.

[35] Gilchrist, 25.

CHAPTER 5

[1] Reynolds, *Alcohol*, 34, 78. Archer, 148.

[2] Archer, 148. See also: Dunn, 11-12.

[3] Keil and Delitzsch, 11:39.

[4] Reynolds, *Alcohol*, 61.

[5] Reynolds, *Alcohol*, 10.

[6] Reynolds, *Alcohol*, 11.

[7] Reynolds, *Alcohol*, 12.

[8] Reynolds, *Alcohol*, 64.

[9] Reynolds, *Alcohol*, 11-14, 63-64.

[10] Reynolds, *Biblical*, 13.

[11] Reynolds, *Biblical*, 14-15.

[12] Reynolds, *Biblical*, 15.

[13] Reynolds, *Biblical*, 7.

[14] Reynolds, *Alcohol*, 10, 30.

[15] Reynolds, *Alcohol*, 12.

[16] Alexander, 1:139. See also: Plumptre, 4:431; Keil and Delitzsch, 1:178.

[17] Reynolds, *Biblical*, 63. For a discussion

of alcohol-as-poison, see the Chapter 7 section titled "Alcohol and Health"

[18] Reynolds, *Biblical,* 64.

[19] Morris, 162.

[20] Morris, 162.

[21] Seeseman, 5:162.

CHAPTER 6

[1] See, for instance, Sanday, 7:258.

[2] Sanday, 7:258.

[3] Gingrich and Danker, 115.

[4] Thayer, 80.

[5] Dana and Mantey, 98.

[6] Sanday, 7:258. See also: Murray, 2:175.

[7] Arndt and Gingrich, 277.

[8] Thayer, 225.

[9] Murray, 11:176. See also: Jamieson, Fausett and Brown, 2:255.

[10] Arndt and Gingrich, 453.

[11] Murray, 2:176.

[12] Paul has not shifted his focus from the weak to the strong between verses 3 and 4. See: Murray, 11:176; Sanday, 7:259.

[13] Matt. 18:15ff; 1 Cor. 5:1-5; Gal. 6:1.

[14] Murray, 2:176.

[15] Sanday, 7:259.

[16] Lenski, 818.

[17] Murray, 11:178; Lenski, 821.

[18] That Paul is not here referring to the weekly recurring sabbath is evident based on the analogy of Scripture: (1) The sabbath is a creational ordinance of perpetual obligation, Gen. 2:1-2; (2) the sabbath is one of the ten fundamental laws in the Decalogue, Ex. 20:8-11; (3) Paul observes the weekly sabbath, 1 Cor. 16:1-2; Acts 20:7 (in its New Testament form); (4) a similarity exists between this passage and those of Gal. 4:10 and Col. 2:16-17, which obviously refers to the ceremonial festal days of Old Covenant Israel.

[19] Stahlin, "Skandalon," 7:355.

[20] Stahlin, "Proskomma," 6:749.

[21] For detail of Israel's first century plight, see Chapter 1 in Ice and Gentry, *The Great Tribulation: Past or Future?*

[22] Thayer, 547.

[23] Stahlin, "Proskomma," 6:753.

[24] Stahlin, "Skandalon," 7:353.

[25] Stahlin, "Skandalon," 7:353.

[26] Stahlin, "Skandalon," 7:341.

[27] Arndt and Gingrich, 760.

[28] Thayer, 577.

[29] Stahlin, "Skandalon," 7:345.

[30] Stahlin, "Skandalon," 7:346.

[31] Murray, 2:188-189.

[32] Reynolds, *Alcohol,* 30.

[33] O'Brien and Chafetz, ix.

[34] Gilchrist, 31-32.

[35] Arndt and Gingrich, 483.

[36] Murray, 2:190-191.

[37] We may insist upon this apart from any conjectural parallelism: (1) There is an obvious close relationship between v. 15a and v. 15c, regardless of a formal structure. (2) The context suggests the stronger meaning of the verb *lupeo*. (3) The following context indicates the weaker Christian is "torn down," v. 20. To be "sad" is not equivalent to being "torn down."

[38] Arndt and Gingrich, 94.

[39] Thayer, 64.

[40] Thayer, 64. See also: Arndt and Gingrich, 94.

[41] Charles Hodge, 424. See also: A. A. Hodge, 544ff; Dabney, 697ff; Berkhof, 397.

[42] Metzger, 532.

[43] See: Sider, 25, 42-44. See also: Brown, *In the Human Interest;* Freudenberger and Minus, Cauthen, 35ff.

[44] Blass and DeBrunner, 174.

45 Lenski, 849.

46 Jamieson, Fausset and Brown, 2:256.

47 Lenski, 850. Hodge, *First Epistle to the Corinthians,* 166; Jamieson, Fausset and Brown, 2:279.

48 Charles Hodge, *Romans,* 429-430.

49 Charles Hodge, *First Corinthians,* 151.

50 Calvin, 1:842, 843 (at 3:19:11).

CHAPTER 7

1 See discussion in foreword of Adams, *Competent to Counsel.*

2 Bahnsen, *Homosexuality,* 69.

3 Langone, 57.

4 Wilkerson, 36, 77.

5 Reynolds, *Biblical,* 103.

6 Reynolds, *Biblical,* 104.

7 "Doctor warns excess water can cause people to be drunk," *Greenville News* (January 4, 1991). This article was based on a report published in the December 1990 edition of the *Journal of the American Medical Association.*

8 Reynolds, *Alcohol,* 33, 55. Van Impe, Ch 3: "The Destroyer."

9 *Alcohol and Health,* 33.

10 *Alcohol and Health,* 33.

11 *Seventh Special Report,* 119-120.

12 Hennekens.

13 LaPorte, 157.

14 LaPorte, 160.

15 "Beer could be healthful, study reports," *Greenville News* (November 18, 1985).

16 Shapiro, 52.

17 Shapiro, 52.

18 Shapiro, 54.

19 "Alcohol helps the heart," *Greenville News* (April 7, 1997).

20 "Moderate drinking decreases the risk of strokes, new study confirms," *Orange County Register* (January 6, 1999). See also: Sacco, 281:53ff.

21 Sacco, 281:53.

22 McCarthy, 10.

23 Reynolds, *Biblical,* 64.

24 Reynolds, *Biblical,* 88.

25 *Alcohol and Health,* 76.

26 Ford, 137.

27 Reynolds, *Biblical,* 78.

28 Cavendish, 1727.

29 Lindsell, 116.

30 Archer, 149.

31 Bustanoby, 50.

32 Edwards, 2:880.

33 Stein, "Wine"; Patton, 42-45.

34 Brown, Driver and Briggs, 587.

35 Russell, 895.

36 Easton, 4:3087.

37 The Hebrew word for "drink" is *sobe,* which is rare. It denotes a fine wine that can intoxicate. As a matter of fact, it is related to the word *saba* which means "drunkard," (Deut. 21:20; Prov. 23:21; Nah. 1:10).

38 Young, 1:82.

39 Cited in Bustanoby, 41.

REFERENCES USED

Abbott-Smith, G., *A Manual Greek Lexicon of the New Testament* (Edinburgh: T & T Clark 1950).

Adams, Jay E., *Competent to Counsel* (Phillipsburg: Presbyterian and Reformed, 1970).

Alcohol and Health: New Knowledge, Morris E. Chafetz, M.D., Chairman, Task Force, U.S. Dept. of Health, Education and Welfare: National Institute on Alcohol and Alcohol Abuse. *Second Special Report to the U.S. Congress on Alcohol and Health* (Washington, D.C.: U.S. Government Printing Office, 1974).

"Alcohol helps the heart," *Greenville News* (April 7, 1997).

Alexander, J.A., *Commentary on the Prophecies of Isaiah* (Grand Rapids: Zondervan, 1977 [1875]).

Archer, Gleason L., *Encyclopedia of Bible Difficulties* (Grand Rapids: Zondervan, 1982).

Arndt, W. F., and F. W. Gingrich, *A Greek-English Lexicon of the New Testament* (Chicago: University of Chicago Press, 1957).

Bahnsen, Greg L., *Homosexuality: A Biblical View* (Grand Rapids: Baker, 1978).

Bahnsen, Greg L., *Van Til's Apologetic: Readings and Analysis* (Phillipsburg: Presbyterian and Reformed, 1998).

Barabas, Steven, "Lees," *The Zondervan Pictorial Encyclopedia of the Bible*, Merrill C. Tenney and Steven Barabas, eds. (Grand Rapids: Zondervan, 1976).

Barbour, Scott, ed., *Alcohol: Opposing Viewpoints* (San Diego: Greenhaven, 1997).

"Beer could be healthful, study reports," *Greenville News* (November 18, 1985).

Behm, Johannes, *Theological Dictionary of the New Testament*, Gerhard Kittel, ed. (Grand Rapids: Eerdmans, 1967).

Berkhof, Louis, *Systematic Theology* (Grand Rapids: Eerdmans, 1972 [1941]).

Blass, F. and A. DeBrunner, *A Greek Grammar of the New Testament and Other Early Christian Literature* (Chicago: University of Chicago Press, 1961).

Brown, Francis, S. R. Driver and C. A. Briggs, *Hebrew and English Lexicon of the Old Testament* (Oxford: Clarendon, 1972).

Brown, Lester R., *In the Human Interest* (New York: Norton, 1974).

Buschel, Friedrich, *Theological Dictionary of the New Testament*, Gerhard Kittel, ed. (Grand Rapids: Eerdmans, 1967).

Bustanoby, Andre S., *The Wrath of Grapes: Drinking and the Church Divided* (Grand Rapids: Baker, 1987).

Calvin, John, *Institutes of the Christian Religion* (Philadelphia: Westminster Press, 1960).

Cauthen, Kenneth, *Christian Biopolitics* (Nashville: Abingdon, 1971).

Cavendish, Marshall, *Illustrated Encyclopedia of Family Health* (1984, vol. 16), 1727.

Chafetz, Morris E., *Liquor: The Servant of Man* (Toronto: Little, Brown, 1965).

Clarke, Adam, *Clarke's Commentary* (Nashville: Abingdon, n.d.).

Dabney, Robert L., *Lectures in Systematic Theology* (Grand Rapids:Zondervan, 1972 [1878]).

Dalman, G., *Arbeir v. Sitte in Palastma*, iv (1935).

Dana, H. E. and Julius R. Mantey, *A Manual Grammar of the Greek New Testament* (Toronto: Macmillan, 1955).

Davidson, Benjamin, *The Analytical and Hebrew and Chaldee Lexicon* (Grand Rapids: Zondervan, 1970).

Davis, John D., "Wine," *Illustrated Davis Bible Dictionary* (Nashville: Royal Publishers, 1973 [1924]).

"Doctor warns excess water can cause people to be drunk,"*Greenville News* (January 4, 1991).

Dunn, Jerry G., *The Christian in a Drinking Society* (Lincoln: Back to the Bible, 1974).

Easton, Burton Scott, "Wine," *International Standard Bible Encyclopedia*, James Orr and John L. Nuelson, eds. (Grand Rapids: Eerdmans, 1929).

Edersheim, Alfred, *The Life and Times of Jesus the Messiah* (Grand Rapids: Eerdmans, 1972).

Edersheim, Alfred, *The Temple: Its Ministry and Services* (Grand Rapids: Eerdmans, 1958).

Edwards, D. Miall, "Drunkenness," *International Standard Bible Encyclopedia*, James Orr and John L. Nuelson, eds. (Grand Rapids: Eerdmans, 1929).

Ellicott, John Charles, ed., "The Four Gospels," *Ellicott's Commentary on the Whole Bible* (Grand Rapids: Zondervan, 1954).

Ewing, Charles Wesley, *The Bible and Its Wines* (Denver: National Prohibition Foundation, 1985).

Fitzsimmonds, F.S., "Wine," *The New Bible Dictionary*, 2nd ed., J. D. Douglas, *et al.*, eds. (Downers Grove: InterVarsity, 1982).

Fleming, Alice, *Alcohol: The Delightful Poison* (New York: Delacorte, 1975).

Ford, Gene, *The French Paradox & Drinking for Health* (San Francisco: Wine Appreciation Guild, 1993).

Frame, John M., "The Problem of Theological Paradox," *Foundations of Christian Scholarship*, Gary North ed. (Vallecito: Ross House, 1976).

Freisen, Garry and J. Robin Maxson, *Decision Making and the Will of God: A Biblical Alternative to the Traditional View* (Portland: Multnomah, 1980).

Freudenberger, C. Dean and Paul M. Minus, Jr., *Christian Responses in a Hungry World* (Nashville: Abingdon, 1976).

Gentry, Kenneth L., Jr., *The Christian and Alcoholic Beverages: A Biblical Perspective* (Grand Rapids: Baker, 1986). This is the first edition of the present re-titled and expanded work.

Gentry, Kenneth L., Jr., *The Greatness of the Great Commission: The Christian Enterprise in a Fallen World,* 2nd ed. (Tyler: Institute for Christian Economics, 1994).

Gentry, Kenneth L., Jr. and Stephen M. Reynolds, "Does Scripture Permit Us to Drink Alcoholic Beverages?" *Antithesis* 2:2 (March-April 1991).

Gilchrist, Paul R., ed., "Study Committee on Beverage Use of Alcohol Report," published in *Documents of Synod* (Lookout Mountain: Reformed Presbyterian Church, Evangelical Synod, 1982).

Gingrich, F. Wilbur and Frederick W. Danker, *A Greek-English Lexicon of the New Testament and Other Early Christian Literature,* 2nd ed. (Chicago: University of Chicago Press, 1979).

Harris, R.L., *The Bible and Wine* (Columbia: Presbyterian Supply House, n.d.).

Harris, R. Laird, Gleason L. Archer, Jr. and Bruce K. Waltke, eds., *Theological Wordbook of the Old Testament* (Chicago: Moody, 1980).

Harrison, R.K., *Encyclopedia of Biblical and Christian Ethics* (Nashville: Thomas Nelson, 1992).

Hendriksen, William, *The Gospel of John* (Grand Rapids: Baker, 1973).

Hennekens, C., *American Heart Association News Release, Abstract No. 1990* (November 19, 1987).

Hodge, A.A., *Outlines of Theology* (Edinburgh: Banner of Truth, 1972 [1860]).

Hodge, Charles, *Commentary on the Epistle to the Romans* (Grand Rapids: Eerdmans, 1972 [1886]).

Hodge, Charles, *Commentary on the First Epistle to the Corinthians* (Grand Rapids: Eerdmans, 1969 [1835]).

Hughes, Philip E., *A Commentary on the Epistle to the Hebrews* (Grand Rapids: Eerdmans, 1977).

Ice, Thomas and Kenneth L. Gentry, Jr., *The Great Tribulation: Past or Future?* (Grand Rapids: Kregel, 1999).

Jamieson, Robert A., R. Fausett and David Brown, *A Commentary, Critical and Explanatory on the Old and New Testaments* (Hartford: Scranton, n.d.).

Keil, C. F. and Franz Delitzsch, *Commentary on the Old Testament* (Grand Rapids: Eerdmans, 1978).

Kerr, C.M., "Drunkenness," *International Standard Bible Encyclopedia*, James Orr and John Nuelson, eds. (Grand Rapids: Eerdmans, 1929).

Kilpatrick, Lester E., "A Review of a Review: *The Christian and Alcoholic Beverages: A Biblical Perspective*," *The Christian Statesman* (May-June 1987).

Kobler, John, *Ardent Spirits* (New York: G. P. Putnam, 1973).

Kuiper, R.B., *The Bible Tells Us So* (Edinburgh: Banner of Truth, 1968).

Langone, John, *Bombed, Buzzed, Smashed or Sober* (Boston: Little, Brown, 1976).

LaPorte, Ronald E., *et al.*, "Alcohol, Coronary Heart Disease, and Total Mortality," *Recent Developments in Alcoholism: Official Publication of the American Medical Society*, Marc Galanter, ed. (New York: Plenum, 1985).

Lee, Francis Nigel, *The Central Significance of Culture* (Nutley: Presbyterian and Reformed, 1976).

Lenski, R.C.H., *The Interpretation of St. Paul's Epistle to the Romans* (Minneapolis: Augsburg, 1961).

Liddell, Henry George and Robert Scott, *A Greek-English Lexicon*, 5th ed. (Oxford: Clarendon, 1864).

Lindsell, Harold, *The World, the Flesh and the Devil* (Washington: Canon Press, 1973).

McCarthy, Raymond, ed., *Drinking and Intoxication* (Glencoe: Free Press, 1959).

Metzger, Bruce Manning, *A Textual Commentary on the Greek New Testament* (London: United Bible Societies, 1971).

Mickelsen, A. Berkeley, *Interpreting the Bible* (Grand Rapids: Eerdmans, 1963).

"Moderate drinking decreases the risk of strokes, new study confirms," *Orange County Register* (January 6, 1999).

Moore, Dunlop, "Wine," *A Religious Encyclopedia of Biblical, Historical, Doctrinal and Practical Theology*, Philip Schaff, ed. (Chicago: Funk and Wagnalls, 1887).

Morris, Henry M., *The Bible Has the Answer* (Nutley: Craig, 1971).

"Moses Stuart," *Encyclopedia of Temperance and Prohibition* (New York: Funk and Wagnalls, 1891).

Murray, John, *The Epistle to the Romans* (Grand Rapids: Eerdmans, 1965).

Nicoll, W. Robertson and J. H. Bernard, eds., *The Expositor's Greek Testament* (Grand Rapids: 1980).

Noll, Mark A. "America's Battle Against the Bottle," *Christianity Today* (January 19, 1979).

North, Gary, *Dominion Covenant: Genesis* (Tyler: Institute for Christian Economics, 1982).

O'Brien, Robert and Morris Chafetz, *The Encyclopedia of Alcoholism* (New York: Facts on File, 1982).

Parkhurst, John, *A Greek and English Lexicon to the New Testament*, 7th ed. (London: Thomas Davison, Whitefriars, 1817).

Patton, William, *Bible Wines: The Laws of Fermentation and the Wines of the Ancients* (Ft. Worth: Star Bible, n.d. [1871]).

Pink, A.W., *An Exposition of Hebrews* (Grand Rapids: Baker, 1954).

Plumptre, E.H., "Isaiah," *Ellicott's Commentary on the Whole Bible*, John Charles Ellicott, ed. (Grand Rapids: Zondervan, n.d.).

Presbyterian Guardian (July-August 1977).

Prevention Plus II: Tools for Creating and Sustaining Drug-Free Communities (Mclean: Office for Substance Abuse Prevention, 1992).

Preisker Herbert, *Theological Dictionary of the New Testament*, Gerhard Kittel, ed. (Grand Rapids: Eerdmans, 1967).

Reynolds, Stephen M., *Alcohol and the Bible* (Little Rock: Challenge Press, 1983).

Reynolds, Stephen M., *The Biblical Approach to Alcohol* (Minneapolis: U. S. Council of the International Organization of Good Templars Alcohol and Drug Abuse Task Force, n.d.). This book appears to have been published sometime around 1988 judging from the latest historical comments found within.

Russell, Emmet, "Wine," *Zondervan Pictorial Bible Dictionary*, Merrill C. Tenney, ed. (Grand Rapids: Zondervan, 1967).

Rushdoony, R. J., *Institutes of Biblical Law*, Vol. I (Nutley: Craig, 1973).

Sacco, Ralph L., *et al.*, "The Protective Effect of Moderate Alcohol Consumption on Ischemic Stroke," *Journal of the American Medical Association* (January 6, 1999).

Sanday, W., "Romans," *Ellicott's Commentary on the Whole Bible*, John Charles Ellicott, ed. (Grand Rapids: Zondervan, 1954).

Schultz, F.W., "Melchizedek," *A Religious Encyclopedia of Biblical, Historical, Doctrinal and Practical Theology*, Philip Schaff, ed. (Chicago: Funk and Wagnalls, 1887).

Schnucker, R.V., "Neo-orthodoxy," *Evangelical Dictionary of Theology*, Walter A. Elwell, ed. (Grand Rapids: Baker, 1984).

Seeseman, Heinrich, *"Oinos,"* *Theological Dictionary of the New Testament*, Gerhard Kittel, ed. (Grand Rapids: Eerdmans, 1967).

Seventh Special Report to the U. S. Congress on Alcohol and Health from the Secretary of Health and Human Services (Rockville: National Institute on Alcohol Abuse and Alcoholism, 990).

Shapiro, Laura, "To Your Health?" *Newsweek* (January 22, 1996).

Shoemaker, Wells, M.D., "Wine, Pregnancy, and Fetal Alcohol Syndrome," *The Moderation Reader* (March-April 1993).

Sider, Ron, *Rich Christians in an Age of Hunger* (Downers Grove: InterVarsity Press, 1977).

Siegel, Mark A., *et al.*, eds., *Illegal Drugs and Alcohol: America's Anguish* (Wylie: Information Plus, 1995).

Spurgeon, Charles H., *The Treasury of David* (New York: Funk and Wagnalls, 1881).

Stahlin, Gustav, "Proskomma," *Theological Dictionary of the New Testament*, Gerhard Friedrich, ed. (Grand Rapids: Eerdmans, 1971).

Stahlin, Gustav, "Skandalon," *Theological Dictionary of the New Testament*, Gerhard Friedrich, ed. (Grand Rapids: Eerdmans, 1971).

Stein, Robert, "Wine Drinking in New Testament Times," *Christianity Today* (June 20, 1975).

Strong, James, *Strong's Exhaustive Concordance of the Bible* (Nashville: Abingdon, 1967 [1890]).

Teachout, Robert P., *The Use of "Wine" in the Old Testament* (Dallas: Dallas Theological Seminary dissertation, 1982).

Thayer, Joseph Henry, *A Greek-English Lexicon of the New Testament* (New York: American Book, 1889).

Tregelles, Samuel Prideaux, *Gesenius' Hebrew and Chaldee Lexicon to the Old Testament Scriptures* (Grand Rapids: Eerdmans, n.d. [1857]).

Trench, Robert, *Notes on the Miracles and Parables of Our Lord* (Old Tappan: Revell, 1953).

Unger, Merrill F., *Unger's Bible Dictionary* (Chicago: Moody Press, 1970).

Van Impe, Jack, *Alcohol: The Beloved Enemy* (Nashville: Thomas Nelson, 1980).

Vos, J.G., *The Separated Life* (Philadelphia: Great Commission Publications, n.d.).

Wilkerson, David, *Sipping Saints* (Old Tappan: Revell, 1978).

Williams, J. Rodman, *The Era of the Spirit* (Plainfield: Logos, 1971).

Williamson, G. I., *Wine in the Bible and the Church* (Phillipsburg: Pilgrim, 1976).

Young, E.J., *The Book of Isaiah* (Grand Rapids: Eerdmans, 1965).

God Gave Wine online: For more information about this title, its author and related subjects, go to godgavewine.com

Also on the Web: oakdown.com